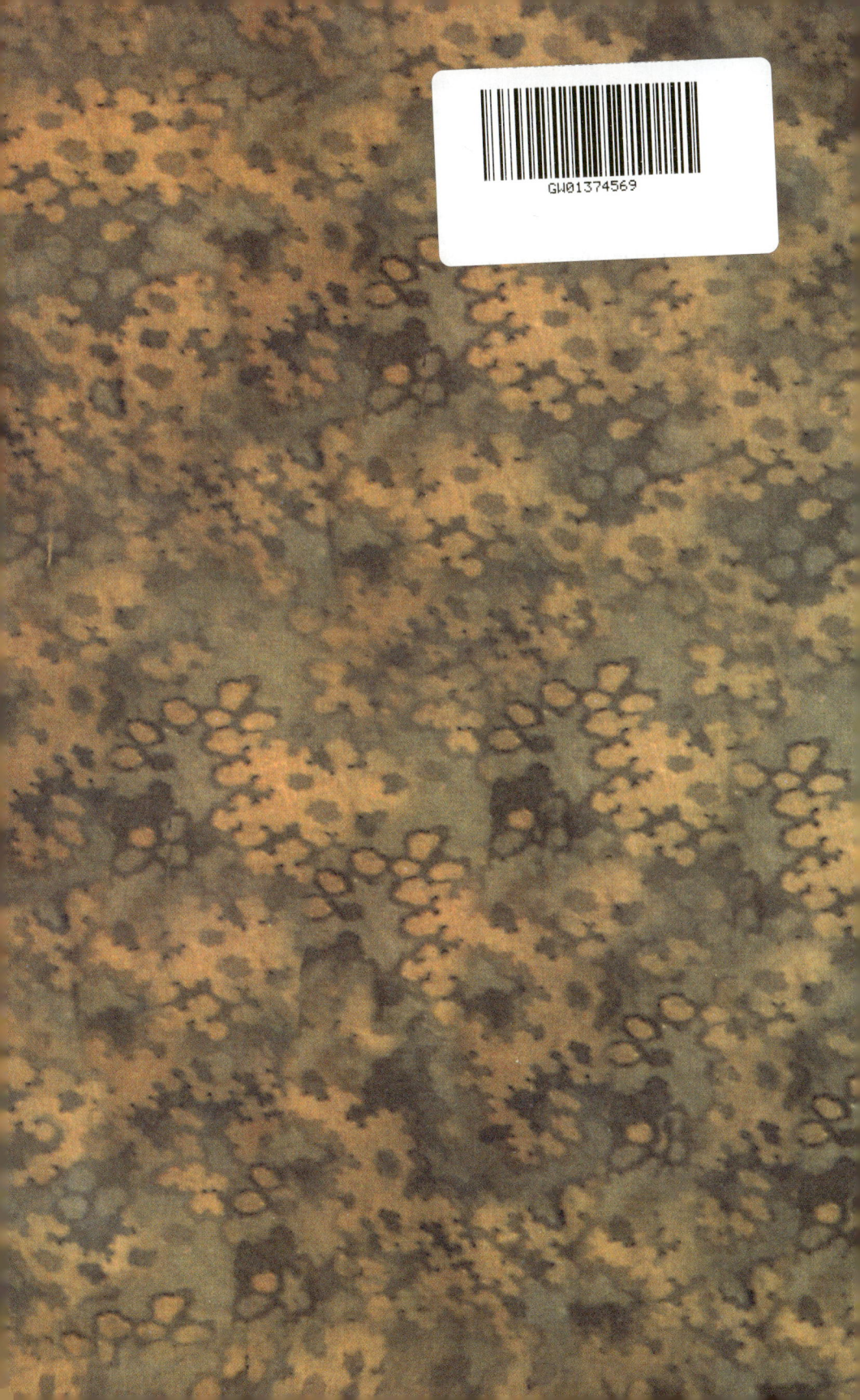

Latvians in the Ordnungspolizei and Waffen-SS
in World War II

Rolf Michaelis

Schiffer Military History
Atglen, PA

Translation from the German by David Johnston.

Book Design by Stephanie Daugherty.

Copyright © 2012 by Schiffer Publishing.
Library of Congress Control Number: 2012942400

All rights reserved. No part of this work may be reproduced or used in any forms or by any means – graphic, electronic or mechanical, including photocopying or information storage and retrieval systems – without written permission from the copyright holder.

The scanning, uploading and distribution of this book or any part thereof via the Internet or via any other means without the permission of the publisher is illegal and punishable by law. Please purchase only authorized editions and do not participate in or encourage the electronic piracy of copyrighted materials.

"Schiffer," "Schiffer Publishing, Ltd. & Design," and the "Design of pen and inkwell" are registered trademarks of Schiffer Publishing, Ltd.

Printed in China.
ISBN: 978-0-7643-4262-2

This book was originally published in German under the title,
Letten in der Ordnungspolizei und Waffen–SS: 1941-1945
by Michaelis-Verlag.

We are interested in hearing from authors with book ideas on related topics.

Published by Schiffer Publishing Ltd.
4880 Lower Valley Road
Atglen, PA 19310
Phone: (610) 593-1777
FAX: (610) 593-2002
E-mail: Info@schifferbooks.com.
Visit our web site at:
www.schifferbooks.com
Please write for a free catalog.
This book may be purchased from the publisher.
Try your bookstore first.

In Europe, Schiffer books are distributed by:
Bushwood Books
6 Marksbury Avenue
Kew Gardens
Surrey TW9 4JF, England
Phone: 44 (0) 20 8392-8585
FAX: 44 (0) 20 8392-9876
E-mail: Info@bushwoodbooks.co.uk.
Visit our website at:
www.bushwoodbooks.co.uk

Contents

Foreword ... 4

Latvia ... 5
Latvians in German Military Service ... 8
   Ordnungspolizei ... 13
      The Latvian *Schutzmannschafts* Battalions ... 14
      Chronology of Battalions ... 14
      The Latvian Volunteer Police Regiments ... 27
      The Latvian SS Grenzschutz
         (Border Defense) Regiments ... 30
   Sicherheitspolizei ... 34
   Latvian SS Volunteer Legion ... 40
      The 15th SS Waffen Grenadier Division (Latvian No.1) ... 43
      The 2nd Latvian SS Volunteer Brigade ... 69
      The 19th SS Waffen Grenadier Division (Latvian No.2) ... 70

Appendix ... 86
   The VI SS Waffen Army Corps (Latvian) ... 86
   The Latvian Field Replacement Depot ... 89
   Command Positions ... 91
   Division Commanders ... 92
      15th SS Waffen Grenadier Division (Latvian No.1) ... 92
      19th SS Waffen Grenadier Division (Latvian No.2) ... 95
   Military Postal Numbers ... 99
   Recipients of Important Decorations ... 100
   Organization of an Infantry Division 43 ... 110
   Rank Comparisons ... 111

Suggested Reading ... 111

Foreword

The Second World War began seventy years ago and caused great damage to many European states. Almost every nation and people was affected and there were countless dramatic fates. If one considers the Baltic States and looks at their eventful history, one is shocked to see how, time and again, small nations were exploited by great powers. This was usually done for economic reasons, for example to obtain ice-free ports for trade or labor and defense forces.

Latvia was also exploited for the latter in 1941 at the hands of Germany. The greater the losses became on the Eastern Front, the more the German leadership tried to find foreign replacements. It made almost no difference whether they were supplements for the labor or military services.

In this regard, on 8 February 1944[1] the chief of SS Headquarters, *SS-Obergruppenführer* Berger, wrote to the Senior SS and Police Commander attached to the Military Commander in France, *SS-Gruppenführer* Oberg, that, *"No German mother weeps for the foreigners who are killed"*. This statement clearly reflects the mindset of one of the influential generals in the Waffen-SS, who alone succeeded in bringing about 230,000 foreigners to the Waffen-SS and thus Germany. Approximately 40,000 of these came from Latvia and from 1943 they joined the Waffen-SS more or less voluntarily or were transferred to the Waffen-SS en masse from the Latvian police units formed after 1941.

This book recounts the histories of these units and shows how and where the Latvians were employed by the German side during the Second World War. The publication cannot reflect the fates of those affected on all sides, however the reader may bear them in mind.

Rolf Michaelis
Berlin, November 2009

---

1 Diary No.106/44 Secret Command Matter dated 8 February 1944.

LATVIA

Latvia – a nation comparable in size to Bavaria, but with just over 1.8 million inhabitants (roughly half that of Berlin) – has had a very eventful history. During the migrations of peoples, Finno-Ugric hunter-gatherers arrived in the area of the eastern Baltic from southern Europe, followed later by nomadic herdsmen from the northern Black Sea region. From these developed the so-called Baltic tribes, the Curonians, Latgalians, Livonians, Selonians and Semigalians. Together with the Balts living farther north, in early histories they were generally referred to as Esthi and the area as Esthland. In the late Middle Ages, after Scandinavians had occupied the northern part of the Baltic, it was called Livland.[2]

At the beginning of the 13th Century missionaries from Germany began the Christianization of the Baltic. To militarily protect this and the no less important economic acquisition of the country, the Brothers of the Sword was formed, which ultimately merged with the Teutonic Knights. Livonia, which encompassed parts of southern Estonia and Latvia, was declared part of the Holy Roman Empire at the Imperial Diet in Augsburg in 1530.

That economic interests have always been cause for war was shown when Ivan the Terrible sent Russian troops into Livonia in 1558 in order to obtain an ice-free port for trade with Western Europe. In the Livonian War that followed, which lasted until 1582, Kurland, Latgalia and Livonia broke away from the weakened Teutonic Order and submitted themselves to the jurisdiction of the stronger Polish-Lithuanian crown. Denmark, Sweden and Poland-Lithuania emerged from the campaign as victors and once again divided Livonia.

The Swedish-Polish War followed in 1600. Though economic interests were involved, it was mainly a religious war between protestant Sweden and catholic Poland. It ended with the Peace of Altmark in 1629. Sweden won and was able to occupy additional parts of Livonia. Poland was left with Courland and Latgalia.

In the so-called Great Nordic War (1700-1721) there were new conflicts in the Baltic between Denmark, Poland, Sweden and Russia, resulting in the end of Swedish hegemony. Estonia and Livonia fell to the Russian Empire. In 1772 the dysfunctional kingdom of Poland-Lithuania was divided ("First Partition of Poland"), as a result of which Latgalia also fell to the Russians. In 1795, after the "Third Partition of Poland", Courland also came under the Russian throne. In 1819 the Tsar abolished the serfdom of the Baltic farmers.[3]

---

2   Esthland was subsequently reduced to the northern part of what today is Estonia.
3   Serfdom had been abolished in the German countries a short time before.

Latvia remained part of Russia until the end of the First World War, even though it had been occupied by Germany since 1914. As part of the German surrender, the German Army had to withdraw from Latvia. After the Russian Revolution the Red Army occupied large areas of the country. The Baltic German Adel established a territorial army made up of remaining German troops and volunteers, and together with the newly-formed Latvian Army it successfully fought the Red Army. After the troops took Riga in May 1919, the German units tried to disarm the Latvian Army, however this led to their own defeat on 23 June. By the summer of 1920 national Latvian troops drove the remnants of the Red Army out of the country. Founded on 18 November 1918, on 11 August 1920 the Latvian government signed a peace treaty with Soviet Russia. In 1934 President Karlis Ulmanis dissolved parliament and established an authoritarian regime. Unlike others of its kind, however, it pursued moderate policies.

Latvia's approximately twenty years of independence ended with the signing of the Hitler-Stalin pact on 23 August 1939. In a secret protocol, Latvia was awarded to the Soviet sphere of influence. On 5 October 1939 there followed a Latvian-Soviet mutual assistance and basing agreement, and on 15 July 1940 the country was incorporated into the Soviet Union as its fifteenth republic. Almost 35,000 anti-communist Latvians were subsequently deported to Siberia, with no opportunity to defend themselves. At the same time, resettlement began of the Baltic Germans, 80% of whom had already left Latvia by 1940.

Within a few days of the attack on the Soviet Union on 22 June 1941, the German military conquered all of Latvia. On 1 September 1941 Latvia was transferred to civilian administration as a general commissariat of the Reich Commissariat *"Ostland"* (*Gauleiter* Lohse). In March 1942 a so-called "consultative council" under General Oskar Dankers was transformed into a domestic administration which took its instructions from the German Commissioner General in Riga (Otto Heinrich Dressler).

The Latvian desire for autonomy was not supported by the Germans. Instead Hitler viewed the country as one of the parts of the USSR occupied by German troops. After the enormous casualties suffered by the German military in the first months of the campaign, however, Germany began looking at the human potential in the occupied eastern territories. Compulsory labor service was introduced in December 1941, followed by compulsory military service in February 1944. By the summer of 1944 the Red Army was again at the Latvian border and by the end of the year it had conquered all parts of the country except Courland. In Courland a military administration was set up on 8 February 1945 under *SS-Gruppenführer* and *Generalleutnant der Polizei* Dr. Hermann Behrends.

At the Allied conferences in Teheran and Yalta, the USA, Great Britain and the USSR regarded Latvia as part of the Soviet Union and so it remained until 1990. Between 1945 and 1949, far more

Rudolfs Bangerskis was born in Taurupe on 21 July 1878 and served in the Latvian Army until he retired on 16 March 1937. On 10 April 1943 he was reactivated as "Inspector of the Latvian SS Volunteer Legion" with the rank of *SS-Gruppenführer*. In this position he was responsible for all administrative matters related to the Latvian SS units. He died in an automobile accident in Oldenburg, Germany on 25 February 1958.

SS-Gruppenführer Bangerskis and the commanding general of the VI SS Waffen Army Corps (Latvian), *SS-Obergruppenführer* Krüger.

than 100,000 Latvians were resettled to Siberia and the country was Russianized. As a result of Gorbachev's policies, efforts to regain the nation's sovereignty culminated in a declaration of independence on 4 May 1990, which was finally recognized by the USSR on 21 August 1991. From 1993 to 1999, the great nephew of Karlis Ulmanis, Guntis Ulmanis, was Latvian president. On 2 April 2004 Latvia joined NATO and on 1 May 2004 the European Union.

Latvians in German Military Service

Approximately 1,800,000 people lived in Latvia in 1941, and of these about 1,500,000 were Latvians. In the summer of 1941 the German military was welcomed as a liberator from communism and many Latvians immediately volunteered to fight against the Red Army. While the military was generally open to the idea of using these men, from a political point of view there was no desire to form larger Latvian combat units. On the other hand, in the summer of 1941 the *Ordnungspolizei* began forming a Latvian auxiliary police force to deal with regular police tasks. At the same time, *Einsatzgruppe* "A" of the *Sicherheitspolizei* (Security Police) and *Sicherheitsdienst* (Security Service) also established an auxiliary security police force which took part in numerous executions of Jews. Finally, in September 1941, a Latvian security battalion was formed from auxiliary police forces. Consisting of five companies, at the end of October 1941 it was moved to northern Russia for use outside Latvia. Four more battalions were formed by January 1942, and two of these were also transferred to Army Group North.

The units designated *Schutzmannschafts* Front Battalions on 6 November 1941 were used to secure lines of communication in the rear and in some cases were employed at the front, while most of the auxiliary police, also designated as *Schutzmannschaften*, carried out normal police duties in Latvia. These ranged from traffic control, combating the black market and fraud to the investigation of murders and the guarding of prisoner of war camps and ghettoes.

Latvian politicians offered to form military units to take part in the struggle against Soviet Russia, but as this offer was closely linked to the country's aspirations for sovereignty, Hitler had no interest. After the three *Schutzmannschafts* Front Battalions deployed in Army Group North's rear area performed well and the German military's losses began to become serious, on 11 February 1942 the Germans began a large-scale recruiting campaign for the *Schutzmannschafts* battalions. The Senior SS and Police Commander *"Ostland"*, *SS-Gruppenführer*

Mikhalkino on the Lovat River.

Members of the 2nd Latvian SS Volunteer Brigade in the spring of 1944 in the area southeast of Ostrov.

Jeckeln, placed an advertisement in the Latvian newspaper *Tevija* (Fatherland). With the support of the self-government, approximately 8,000 volunteers[4] were mustered by May 1942. By the end of the year the bulk of these volunteers were used to form eighteen more battalions (21-28, 266-275). In addition to strong anti-communist sentiments,

---

4   On 24 April 1942 there were already 7,390 Latvians in the battalions.

the volunteers were also motivated by the pay[5], the food, free medical care and benefits for the families of the fallen[6].

When the six-month and one-year enlistments of many *Schutzmannschafts* battalions ran out in the autumn of 1942, the Waffen-SS continued recruiting, in particular for official military service on the German side. The effort was a success, for within a few weeks approximately 4,000 *Schutzmannschafts* members went over to the Latvian SS Volunteer Legion (*Lettische SS-Freiwilligen-Legion*).

At the end of 1942 the enormous German losses on the Eastern Front led to plans to better exploit the defense and labor potential of the three Baltic States, Lithuania, Latvia and Estonia. With a total of about 4.5 million inhabitants and a conscription quota of just 5%, the Baltic Sates alone could have provided 225,000 soldiers for the war against Russia. On 25 February 1943, the 1919 to 1924 age classes were called up for labor service[7], and the draftees were given the choice of serving in the (war) economy or joining the Latvian SS Volunteer Legion.

Of the approximately 70,000 Latvians drafted, about 30% volunteered for military service. Himmler had expected 50,000 volunteers! About 18,000 men were used to form the Latvian SS Volunteer Division (Lettische SS-Freiwillige-Division). It was one of the first three divisions recruited from countries where mobilization of the population had been minimal, following the tragedy at Stalingrad. They were the:

    11th Latvian SS Volunteer Division
    12th Lithuanian SS Volunteer Division[8]
    13th Croatian SS Volunteer Division.

In Latvia this meant that, in addition to the 18,000 men for the division, there was still a contingent of about 12,000 volunteers.

---

5 When used outside their bases in Latvia, members of the Latvian *Schutzmannschaften* received a daily wage which ranged from 3.80 Reichsmark for a simple Schutzmann to 15.50 Reichsmark for a battalion commander.
6 On the death of a Latvian member of the *Schutzmannschaften*, a monthly survivor's pension of between 43 and 144 Reichsmark was paid, depending on rank and age, plus full or half benefits for orphans.
7 Compulsory work was introduced in the occupied eastern areas (including Latvia) on 19 December 1941. This obliged all Latvians between the ages of 18 and 45 to serve in the Reich Commissariat *"Ostland"* in accordance with their ability to work. On 27 August 1942 the age limits were removed – extending compulsory work to include children and old men.
8 After the Lithuanians showed little response to Waffen-SS recruitment and Himmler ultimately questioned the reliability of the country, on 2 December 1943 the OKW war diarist wrote: *"The Reichsführer-SS* has decided not to form a Lithuanian unit. The army has only drafted Lithuanians to serve in construction battalions."

Of these, approximately 4,000 were assigned to the 2nd Latvian SS Volunteer Brigade, 4,000 to replacement training units and 4,000 to the *Schutzmannschaften*. On 18 August 1943 the *Schutzmannschaften*, which were later renamed police battalions (*Polizei*-Bataillonen), had a total strength of just under 10,000 men.

Another wave of call-ups took place in October 1943, as a result of which a total of about 5,600 men from the 1914 to 1924 age classes were drafted for the Latvian SS Volunteer Legion. Just a month later the 1925 age class was called up for military service. The OKW war diarist noted on 2 December 1943:

> "In Latvia ten age classes have been called up, this following a registration action under the compulsory work law; the results were poorer than expected, however, as the Latvian draft registration system per se is inefficient and many draftees try to avoid service due to personal motives and the effects of enemy propaganda. In order to exploit the manpower of Latvia, fifty recruiting offices have been set up, each with a representative of the armed forces. The SS, the GBA, the Reichsbahn, the nation's economic sector and other participating agencies submitted their requirements. How the Latvians brought in by the new measures are to be used has not yet been completely sorted out...
>
> In general the Estonians have performed very well, the Latvians well, the Lithuanians poorly and the White Ruthenians very poorly.
>
> The OKW is now informing the participating parties that the *Führer* has passed the task of conscripting the Estonians and Latvians fit for military service to *the Reichsführer-SS*. For this purpose SS recruiting detachments are being set up in Reval and Riga. These will have the same authority as a German military district command."

On 7 February 1944 general mobilization was declared in Latvia. This also affected the 1908 to 1913 age classes. Of the roughly 70,000 men who were mustered by April 1944, approximately 10,000 fit candidates were taken into the Waffen-SS and 17,000 into the six SS Border Defense Regiments[9] (*SS-Grenzschutz-Regimenter*) then being formed. Other contingents joined the Luftwaffe, the police and construction battalions. In addition, all 17- to 60-year-olds not yet actively employed were drafted into the Selbstschutz, or self-defense force, whose role would be similar to that of the later German Volkssturm.

---

9 The SS Border Defense Regiments were formed within the framework of the *Ordnungspolizei*.

On 1 July 1944 12,159 Latvian volunteers were serving in German units as so-called "auxiliary volunteers" (Hilfswillige) and "battle helpers" (Kampfhelfer). One such volunteer was Edgars Gerdens, who served in the Luftwaffe, initially in the 5th Company of Anti-Aircraft Searchlight Replacement Battalion 43 and from 8 November 1944 in the 4th Company of Parachute Supply Battalion 21.

On 1 July 1944 a total of more than 87,000 Latvians[10] were serving on the German side:

> 11,537 men in the 15th SS Waffen Grenadier Division (Latvian No. 1)
> 19.909 men in the 19th SS Waffen Grenadier Division (Latvian No. 2)
> 12,118 men in the six Border Defense Regiments
> 14,884 men in the police battalions and regiments
> 12,159 men as foreign auxiliaries or combat helpers (Kampfhelfer) in German divisions
> 10,585 men in various German formations like the Todt Organization and the National-Socialist Motor Corps (NSKK)
> 5,240 men in local Latvian self-defense units
> 628 men in air force units

In August 1944 the 1926 and 1927 age classes were mobilized and older age classes were called up. All of those from the 1927 age class found fit for service were assigned to the flak arm as Luftwaffe auxiliaries.

ORDNUNGSPOLIZEI

The German *Ordnungspolizei*'s responsibilities included general police law, police criminal law and criminal proceedings, as well as traffic and commercial law. In addition, from 1939 entire units were used to safeguard annexed and occupied territories. Beginning in 1941, so-called foreign *Schutzmannschaften* (police units) were set up under the command of the *Ordnungspolizei* in the occupied areas of the USSR to perform similar duties. Of particular importance were the so-called *Schutzmannschaften*-Bataillonen (police battalions), which were used to guard captured areas against partisans and on various occasions were also used at the front. Under the *Sicherheitspolizei*, on various occasions they also took part in actions against Jews.

Following the decree of 9 December 1943, most Baltic *Ordnungspolizei* units officially dropped the name *Schutzmannschaften*. From then on they were administered as police units, for example Latvian Police Battalion 206.

---

10 Between 1941 and 1945 a total of about 100,000 Latvians served on the German side in a military role, equal to just over 5% of the population. Interestingly, this figure is the same as the number of men offered to Germany by Latvian politicians in 1941 in exchange for Germany's acceptance and acknowledgement of Latvian sovereignty. The absolute figure was equivalent to about six 16,000-man infantry divisions.

The Latvian Schutzmannschafts-Bataillonen

Approximately 20,000 Latvians served in the *Schutzmannschafts-Bataillonen*. A total of five battalions were formed in 1941, of which three were integrated into the 2nd Latvian SS Volunteer Brigade.[11] One battalion was disbanded in 1943 and the rest were absorbed by Police Battalion 25. In 1944 the last of these battalions came under the command of Latvian Volunteer Police Regiment 1.

Eighteen battalions were formed in 1942. These units, designated *Schutzmannschafts* Replacement Battalions, were given the same numbers as the *Schutzmannschafts* Front Battalions formed in 1941.[11] Six of the 1942 battalions became part of the Latvian SS Volunteer Legion in 1943. Two battalions were used in the formation of the Latvian volunteer police regiments in 1943, nine were disbanded between 1942 and 1944, and one was absorbed by the army. Thus at the end of 1942 there was a total of 22 *Schutzmannschafts* battalions, two of which were already attached to the Waffen-SS [2nd SS Motorized Infantry Brigade]. The strengths of the various battalions varied widely, but on average they had about 400 men, and at the end of 1942 there were about 8,000 Latvians serving in the *Schutzmannschafts* battalions.

Eighteen battalions were formed in 1943, of which nine were integrated into the Latvian Volunteer Police Regiments 1 to 3 then being formed. One battalion went directly into the 2nd Latvian SS Volunteer Brigade and five were disbanded, some soon after they were established. For the first time the minority Latgalians were used to form units, two construction battalions. Of the eighteen units formed in 1943, just one remained an independent police unit until the end of the war.

In 1944 another five battalions were formed, four of which were construction battalions made up of Latgalians. The fifth 1944 battalion, a police battalion, existed until the end of the war. It was attached to the 19th SS Waffen Grenadier Division (Latvian No.2) but was not integrated into the division formation.

Chronology of the Battalions

***Schutzmannschafts* Front Battalion 16** was established as the 1st Latvian Security Battalion in Riga on 4 September 1941, and on 20 October of that year it was placed at the disposal of Army Group North. The battalion was deployed in the Dno area (approx. 90 km east of Pskov) in the 16th Army's rear army area until the end of December 1941, after which it guarded the rear area of the X Army Corps south of Lake Ilmen near Staraya Russa. When the Red Army

---

11 In addition, units primarily tasked with guard duties were called *Schutzmannschafts* Guard Battalions.

The uniforms worn by the Latvian *Schutzmannschaften* varied widely. Initially they were supposed to wear the prewar uniforms of the Latvian Police and Army with Latvian rank badges (see table below). These uniforms were supplemented by articles of Red Army uniform. A white armband with the script *Schutzmannschafts* was only worn in the beginning (see photo above). Due to the formation of numerous units and wear and tear on uniforms in service, as time went by Dutch, Danish and even German uniforms were issued to the *Schutzmannschaften*, which presented a diverse picture as a result.

Ranks of the Latvian *Schutzmannschaften*

Kareivis	1 diagonal bar on the collar tab	*Schütze*
Dizkareivis	same plus 1 vertical ba	*Obergefreiter*
Kapralis	same plus 2 vertical bars	*Stabsgefreiter*
Serzants	same plus 3 vertical bars	*Unteroffizier*
Virsseerzants	same plus 1 broad vertical bar	*Feldwebel*
Virsniekavietnieks	same plus 1 broad vertical bar and 1 star	*Stabsfeldwebel*
Leitnants	same plus 1 star	*Leutnant*
Virsleitnants	same plus 2 stars	*Oberleutnant*
Kapteinis	same plus 3 stars	*Hauptmann*
Majors	same plus 1 large star	*Major*
Pulkvezleitnants	same plus 2 large stars	*Oberstleutnant*
Pulkvedis	same plus 3 large stars	*Oberst*

launched its big offensive on 8 January 1942, the unit was renamed *Schutzmannschafts* Front Battalion 16 and saw action at the front. At the beginning of 1943 the battalion moved to the Krasnoye Selo area where it initially formed the III Battalion of the Latvian Legion. At that time the battalion's strength was bolstered by about 80 men from *Schutzmannschafts* Battalion 276. The battalion also received 300 German rifles, 12 mortars and seven infantry guns. In the heavy defensive fighting that followed, NCO Bogdanov became the first Latvian to be decorated with the Iron Cross, First Class. At the end of April 1943 the unit became the I Battalion of SS Volunteer Regiment 1 (Latvian SS Volunteer Brigade).

Schutzmannschafts **Replacement Battalion 16** was formed in Riga and Bolderaja on 21 March 1942 and on 18 May of the same year was renamed *Schutzmannschafts* Battalion 266.

Schutzmannschafts **Front Battalion 17** was formed in Riga on 21 December 1941. With a strength of 10 officers, 47 non-commissioned officers and 279 enlisted men, it was transferred to Lepel in the sector controlled by Senior SS and Police Commander "Russia Center". In May 1942 the unit was ordered into the Dnepropetrovsk area, in the process of which the 4th Company left the battalion and was sent to the Senior Quartermaster of Army Group North as East Guard Company 652 (Latvian)[12]. The other three companies' assignments included guarding the construction of Through Road IV[13] and the associated labor camps, including in the Ovruch area. In the course of various restructurings associated with the formation of the Latvian SS Volunteer Legion, in May 1943 the battalion was disbanded and elements were absorbed by *Schutzmannschafts* Battalion 25.

Schutzmannschafts **Replacement Battalion 17** was formed in Kraslava (Kreslau in German, approx. 50 km east of Dvinsk) on 18 March 1942 and on 18 May was renamed *Schutzmannschafts* Battalion 267.

Schutzmannschafts **Front Battalion 18** (Military Postal Number 39 250) was formed in Riga on 4 September 1941 as the 2nd Latvian Security Battalion. After it was renamed *Schutzmannschafts* Front Battalion 18, in May 1942 it moved into the sector of the Senior SS and Police Commander "Russia Center" with 14 officers, 86 non-commissioned officers and 501 enlisted men. Stationed in the area southwest of Minsk near Stolpce, the battalion took part in many anti-partisan operations (e.g. "Operation Hamburg" in the Slonim area in

---

12 It was one of the few Latvian units that was part of the army. All others belonged to the *Ordnungspolizei*, Waffen-SS or Luftwaffe.

13 Planned by the Todt Organization, Through Road IV ran from Przemsyl through Lvov to Ternopol and was built in part by Jewish forced laborers who were housed in about 15 work camps along the supply road.

Areas of operations of the Latvian *Schutzmannschafts* battalions in the summer of 1942.

January 1943). When the Latvian SS Volunteer Brigade was formed in May 1943 it became III Battalion, SS Volunteer Regiment 2.

***Schutzmannschafts* Replacement Battalion 18** was formed in Libau on 18 March 1942 and on 18 May was renamed *Schutzmannschafts* Battalion 268.

Schutzmannschafts Front Battalion 19 (Military Postal Number 15 205[14]) was formed in Riga on 16 December 1941 and in May 1942 was transferred into the Krasnoye Selo area with a strength of 512 men. Together with *Schutzmannschafts* Front Battalion 21, it was deployed in the siege ring around Leningrad under the 2nd SS Motorized Infantry Brigade. At the beginning of February 1943 the battalion became the Latvian Legion's II Battalion. Then in April 1943 it was issued German uniforms and equipment and was taken into the Latvian SS Volunteer Brigade as II Battalion, SS Volunteer Regiment 1. As part of this brigade it was transferred to the Volkhov front.

Schutzmannschafts Replacement Battalion 19 was formed from former Latvian border guard units on 18 March 1942, however on 18 May it was renamed *Schutzmannschafts* Battalion 269.

Schutzmannschafts Guard Battalion 20 was formed in Riga on 4 September 1941 as the 3rd Latvian Security Battalion and was employed to guard important bridges and installations plus the Jewish ghetto. In January 1942 it was renamed *Schutzmannschafts* Guard Battalion 20. In 1944, with the Red Army at the gates of Riga, the battalion was ordered to Libau. From there it was evacuated by sea to Danzig on 25 October, along with the staff of the Inspector of the Latvian SS Volunteer Legion (*SS-Gruppenführer* Bangerskis). There it was attached to Latvian Volunteer Police Regiment 1 as its IV Battalion.

Schutzmannschafts Replacement Battalion 20 (Military Postal Number 47 162) was formed in Abrene (prior to 1938 Jaunlatgale; Russian Pytalovo, approx. 100 km SW of Pskov) on 30 July 1941 as the Latvian (Pioneer) Security Battalion. On 18 May 1942 it was renamed *Schutzmannschafts* Battalion 270.

Schutzmannschafts Front Battalion 21 (Military Postal Number 45 849) was formed in Libau on 25 February 1941, and in May it was ordered into the Krasnoye Selo area with 18 officers, 84 non-commissioned officers and 487 enlisted men. It and *Schutzmannschafts* Front Battalion 19 were attached to the 2nd SS Motorized Infantry Brigade taking part in the siege of Leningrad. In February 1943 it became the I Battalion of the Latvian Volunteer Legion and in mid-May 1943 the I Battalion of the 1st SS Volunteer Regiment.

Schutzmannschafts Front Battalion 22 (Military Postal Numbers 19 620 and 09 939 as Latvian Police Battalion 22) was formed in Riga and Bolderaja on 25 February 1942 and in July of that year was transferred to Warsaw in the Generalgouvernement. There the battalion carried out numerous guard duties outside the ghetto and took part in the deportations between August and October 1942. The battalion was then ordered to Stalino. From there it moved farther west into the Zhitomir area. In

---

14 Interestingly, in the summary of military postal numbers the battalion was called *Schutzmannschafts-Abteilung 19* instead of *Schutzmannschafts-Bataillon 19*.

Zaphorozhye on 1 July 1943 it reported 368 men on strength. At the end of 1943 the battalion was ordered back to Latvia, and on 7 February 1944 it became the I Battalion of Latvian Volunteer Police Regiment 2. What remained of the unit was evacuated to Germany in October 1944.

Schutzmannschafts **Front Battalion 23** (Military Postal Numbers 56 833 and 15 576 in 1945) was formed in Bolderaja on 25 February 1942. On 12 May 1942 it was ordered into the Reich Commissariat "Ukraine" with 15 officers, 67 non-commissioned officers and 423 enlisted men. In addition to general security duties the battalion helped guard Through Road IV and the associated labor camps. In the late summer of 1943 the battalion received orders to move to Kerch in the Crimea. At the end of January 1944, when its strength was just 178 men, it was brought into the Rovno area during the retreat by Police Battle Group "Prützmann"[15]. On 8 July 1944 it was ordered into the Yablonka-Krasne area. What was left of the battalion was then moved to the 16th Army and attached to the 215th Infantry Division. At the beginning of 1945 the unit, still designated a *Schutzmannschafts-Bataillon*, was given a new Military Postal Number and was deployed in Courland until the end of the war.

Schutzmannschafts **Front Battalion 24** (Military Postal Number 40 019) was formed in Libau on 1 March 1942 and in May of that year was transferred to the Stankov area (approx. 40 km SW of Minsk) in White Russia. At the end of October 1942 the battalion was transferred to the Leningrad front and attached to Infantry Regiment 380 near Peterhof. When its Latvian members' enlistments ran out on 31 December 1942, the Germans encouraged them to extend. Eighty percent of the men refused at first, as they had been disappointed by their experiences in service to date. The had not been given Latvian uniforms as promised, instead receiving a mixture of mainly captured items of uniform, and had been given no leave since signing up..Most nevertheless appear to have extended their enlistments, for on 11 April 1943 the battalion was taken out of action and moved into the Pushkin area. From there it was ordered to the Volkhov and was renamed I Battalion, SS Volunteer Regiment 2, part of the Latvian SS Volunteer Brigade.

Schutzmannschafts **Front Battalion 25** (Military Postal Number 41 246) was formed in Libau on 6 March 1942 and in July of that year was transferred to the Korosten – Ovruch area to help safeguard the harvest and guard Through Road IV. On 1 July 1943 the battalion had 659 men on strength. At the beginning of 1944 it was ordered back to Latvia, where it was absorbed by Latvian Volunteer Police Regiment 2.

---

15 Police units of the Supreme SS and Police Commander "Ukraine", *SS-Obergruppenführer* Prützmann, were combined to form a battle group and initially placed under the *Wehrmacht* Commander "Ukraine". Together with the 454th Security Division, at heavy cost it attempted to delay the Red Army's advance toward the *Generalgouvernement*.

Schutzmannschafts Front Battalion 26 (Military Postal Number 42 181) was formed in Tukkum on 6 March 1942, In July the unit was transferred to Begoml (approx. 100 km NE of Minsk), where strong partisan units had formed in the surrounding areas. In December 1942, during the Russian winter offensive, it was ordered to the XXXVIII Army Corps on the Novgorod front. The battalion was attached to the 1st Luftwaffe Field Division until mid-March 1942. On 19 April 1943 it became part of the Latvian SS Volunteer Brigade as II Battalion, SS Volunteer Regiment 2. As a result the *Schutzmannschaften*, previously armed with a mix of Russian and German weapons and clothed in Latvian and German police and air force uniforms, were issued standard German uniforms and equipment. At the end of 1943 the unit was sent replacements, after which it was moved to the Volkhov.

Schutzmannschafts Front Battalion 27 was formed in Riga and Magnisholm on 14 March 1942 and subsequently moved to Grishino in the Ukraine (approx. 150 km E of Dnepropetrovsk near Krasnoarmeysk). In July 1942 it was ordered to Krivoy Rog to guard Through Road IV (which included the labor camps set up for the building of the road). From 13 February to 5 March 1943 the battalion was attached to the 19th Panzer Division in the Izyum area. It subsequently saw action at the front with the 3rd Panzer Division and in April 1943 was disbanded on account of heavy casualties. The survivors joined the Latvian SS Volunteer Brigade,

Schutzmannschafts Front Battalion 28 (Military Postal Number 43 965) was formed in Libau on 9 March 1942 and in September was transferred to Krivoy Rog (to guard Through Road IV). Reduced from four to three companies in March 1943, in July the battalion was ordered back to Latvia. It was disbanded on 7 September 1943 and its remaining personnel were absorbed by the Latvian SS Volunteer Brigade.

Schutzmannschafts Guard Battalion 266 was created on 18 May 1942 by renaming *Schutzmannschafts* Replacement Battalion 16. Renamed Latvian Police Battalion 266 in 1943, until October of that year the battalion was deployed on guard duty in the Bolderaja area on the Gulf of Finland north of Riga. It was eventually transferred to Germany, where it was incorporated into the Latvian Field Replacement Depot.

Schutzmannschafts Battalion 267 was created on 18 May 1942 by renaming *Schutzmannschafts* Replacement Battalion 17 and until November was quartered in Kraslava (German Kreslau, approx. 50 km E of Dvinsk). After the Red Army attacked and encircled Velikiye Luki on 24 November 1942, *Schutzmannschafts* Battalion 267 was thrown into the hotly-contested area held by the 9th Army. After the fighting ended, the battalion remained in Army Group Center's sector for a short time and on 1 June 1943 (after the one-year service commitment expired) was disbanded. Some of its personnel joined the Latvian SS Volunteer Legion.

Members of the Latvian *Schutzmannschafts* Battalions, deployed on the Eastern Front since the winter of 1941-42, are decorated with the Iron Cross, Second Class. Most are wearing Latvian uniforms and rank badges, but have German helmets and winter clothing.

A Serzants (*Unteroffizier*) uses field glasses to scan the terrain in front of his position.

As a rule, the *Schutzmannschafts* battalions not deployed at the front were issued Czech (see photo left) or Dutch helmets.

***Schutzmannschafts* Front Battalion 268** was created on 18 May 1942 by renaming *Schutzmannschafts* Replacement Battalion 18 and was located in Libau until July. It was then transferred into the Dnepropetrovsk area, where it was employed in a security role (in part associated with Through Road IV). On 1 July 1943 the battalion had 309 men and on 3 February 1944 was disbanded. Its remaining personnel joined the Latvian SS Volunteer Legion.

***Schutzmannschafts* Guard Battalion 269** was created on 18 May 1942 by renaming *Schutzmannschafts* Replacement Battalion 19 and was used in border defense and guard duties in Latvia. It was disbanded in May 1943 when the Latvian SS Volunteer Legion was formed.

***Schutzmannschafts* Front Battalion 270** (Military Postal Number 47 162) was created on 18 May 1942 by renaming *Schutzmannschafts* Replacement Battalion 20 and was specially trained in the pioneer role. It was attached to the 281st Security Division and single companies were also detached for short periods to the II Army Corps. In September 1942 the battalion was transferred into the area of the Commander of *Ordnungspolizei* "Russia South". In July 1944 it was renamed East Pioneer Battalion 672 (Latvian) and became part of the army. Attached to the commander of Rear Army Area North, the pioneer battalion was in Courland when the war ended.

***Schutzmannschafts* Front Battalion 271** was formed in Libau on 1 July 1942 and then transferred to the Minsk area in White Russia. It took part in many anti-partisan operations (e.g. "Operations Hamburg" and "Altona" in the Slonim area in December 1942, and "Operation Harvest Festival" beginning 15 January 1943). The orders issued prior to these operations were clear: *"Attack and destroy the bandits. Every bandit, Jew, Gypsy and suspected partisan is to be considered hostile. The seizure of agricultural products is accorded special importance."*[16] From 21 May to 22 June 1943 the battalion took part in "Operation Kottbus" and from 15 July to 5 August 1943 in "Operation Hermann" in the Nalibocki Forest area. In the summer of 1944 it was ordered into the main line of resistance in Latvia between Sigulda and Dobele. In October 1944 the battalion was attached to theVI SS Waffen Army Corps (Latvian). Employed in the Dzukste area, it saw action near Puces (approx. 20 km SW of Kandava). The remnants of the battalion were absorbed by the Latvian SS Volunteer Legion.

***Schutzmannschafts* Front Battalion 272** was formed in Riga and Bolderaja on 1 July 1942, and in August it was transferred to Warsaw in the *Generalgouvernement* for guard duties. The battalion carried out numerous guard assignments outside the ghetto and participated in the deportations

---

16 From the order issued by *Einsatzgruppe "Griep"* for "Operation Harvest Festival" on 15 January 1943.

between August and October 1942. In October of the year it received orders to release a company for the formation of *Schutzmannschafts* Battalion 274. In April 1943 the battalion, now with three companies, was briefly transferred to Dnepropetrovsk. It was disbanded in May 1943 and its remaining personnel sent to the Latvian SS Volunteer Legion.

Schutzmannschafts **Front Battalion 273** was formed in Ludz on 1 July 1942. It was deployed in the southern border region, where it took part in "Operation Winter Magic" from 19 February to 7 March 1943 under the command of Senior SS and Police Commander *"Lettland"*, *SS-Brigadeführer* Schröder. The battalion was disbanded on 15 July 1943 and its men were absorbed by *Schutzmannschafts* Battalion 276.

Schutzmannschafts **Guard Battalion 274** was supposed to be formed in October 1942 from personnel released by *Schutzmannschafts* Front Battalion 272. In fact, however, just a single company was raised, and this was deployed in Bobruisk until October 1943. Transferred to Polotsk, it saw action until March 1944. The company was then ordered to Riga, where it undertook guard duties until it was disbanded on 30 September 1944.

Schutzmannschafts **Front Battalion 275** was supposed to be formed in Riga in October 1942, but like *Schutzmannschafts* Guard Battalion 274 it consisted of just a single company. The battalion was disbanded on 7 December and its men were transferred to *Schutzmannschafts* Front Battalion 278.

Schutzmannschafts **Front Battalion 276** was formed in Kuldiga (German Goldingen) in January 1943 and deployed on guard duties in Vilaka (near Marienhausen, approx. 100 km SW of Pskov) in the Russian frontier region. In February 1943 the battalion was combined with *Schutzmannschafts* Front Battalions 277, 278 and 312, Motorized Military Police Platoon 10, Flak Platoon "Hatje" and Signals Platoon "Lewinski" to form the approximately 2,500-man-strong Police Battle Group "Knecht" (Oberst der Schutz*polizei* Knecht). In conjunction with Police Battle Group Schröder (SS and Police Commander "Latvia" *SS-Brigadeführer* Schröder), it combated partisans in the Latvian-Russian border region until the end of March 1943. In June 1943 the battalion was attached to Latvian Volunteer Police Regiment 1.

Schutzmannschafts **Front Battalion 277** was formed in Riga in January 1943 and from February 1943 took part in anti-partisan operations in the Kraslava area (approx. 40 km E of Dvinsk). In the summer of that year the battalion was attached to Latvian Volunteer Police Regiment 1.

Schutzmannschafts **Front Battalion 278** was formed in Riga in January 1943 and was initially ordered to Ludza (approx. 25 km E of Rositten), in the Russian border region. In February 1943 it took part in anti-partisan operations in the Kraslava area as part of Police Battle Group "Knecht". At the end of March 1943 the battalion was marched back to Ludza and was again deployed in the border region. Finally it formed the III Battalion in Latvian Volunteer Police Regiment 1.

Schutzmannschafts Front Battalion 279 was formed in Riga effective 4 January 1943 and in February it took part in operations against partisan forces in the Kraslava area as part of Police Battle Group "Knecht". From April to July 1944 the battalion was employed on guard and security tasks in the Zilupe (on the Russian border approx. 50 km SE of Rositten) border region. The battalion was disbanded on 15 July 1943 and its remaining personnel were assigned to Latvian Volunteer Police Regiment 1.

Schutzmannschafts Front Battalion 280 was formed in Bolderaja on 23 January 1943 and transferred to the Zilupe area. In February 1943 the battalion was made part of the approximately 2,000-man-strong Police Battle Group "Schröder" (SS and Police Commander "Latvia" *SS-Brigadeführer* Schröder), which took part in operations against partisans in the Latvian-Russian border region until the end of March 1943. The battalion was disbanded on 9 April 1943.

Schutzmannschafts Front Battalion 281 was formed in Bolderaja on 23 January 1943 and attached to Police Battle Group "Schröder" (see *Schutzmannschafts* Front Battalion 280). The battalion was disbanded on 9 April 1943.

Schutzmannschafts Front Battalion 282 was formed in Riga in March 1943 and was also transferred to Zilupe. It was disbanded in June 1943 during formation of Latvian Volunteer Police Regiment 1. Its remaining manpower was transferred to *Schutzmannschafts* Front Battalion 276.

Schutzmannschafts Front Battalion 283 was formed in July 1942 and existed until autumn 1944. After it was disbanded, its remaining personnel were sent to the Latvian Field Replacement Depot in Danzig.

Latvian Police Battalion 311 was formed in Valmiera (German Wolmar) in May 1943. It guarded the rail line between Meitene and Valka until the beginning of July 1943 and was then disbanded.

Latvian Police Battalion 312 was formed in Dvinsk in May 1943 and in July was absorbed by Latvian Volunteer Police Regiment 1.

Latvian Police Front Battalion 313 (Military Postal Number 39 428) was formed in August 1943 and in November was transferred the Vilna area in Lithuania. It subsequently saw action at Molodechno in White Russia and in mid-December 1943 was attached to Police Battle Group "Jeckeln". It was deployed in the Nevel area with the battle group and in February 1944 was incorporated into Latvian Volunteer Police Regiment 2.

Latgalian *Schutzmannschafts*[17] **Battalion 314** (Military Postal Number 27 288) was formed in April 1944 using Latgalians[18] living

---

17 In contrast to the purely Latvian battalions, which were renamed police battalions in 1943, the Latgalian battalions retained the title *"Schutzmannschaften"*.
18 The Latgalians were a small minority in Latvia who spoke their own language (Latgalian), which in some cases they were permitted to use as the official language in their own regions.

in Latvia and was employed in the construction of positions in Latvia until November 1944.

Latgalian *Schutzmannschafts* Battalion 315 (Military Postal Number) 56 540) was formed in January using Latgalians and was employed as a construction battalion in Latvia until the end of the war.

Latvian Police Battalion 316 (Military Postal Number 36 570) was formed in Riga on 2 August 1943 and was transferred to the Vilnius area for use against Lithuanian partisans. At the end of 1943 the battalion was sent to Battle Group "Jeckeln", which after "Operation Heinrich" was at the front near Nevel. In mid-January 1944 the unit was attached to the 263rd Infantry Division and one month later to the 83rd Infantry Division. The battalion ultimately became part of Latvian Volunteer Police Regiment 2.

Latvian Police Battalion 317 (Military Postal Number 09 505) was formed in Riga and Bolderaja on 18 October 1943. After being used to guard the Zilupe area, on 14 February 1944 it became part of Latvian Volunteer Police Regiment 3.

Latvian Police Battalion 318 (Military Postal Number 11 441) was formed in Riga on 25 October 1943 and until 14 February 1944 was deployed on the Russian border in the Ludza area (approx. 25 km E of Rositten). It was subsequently incorporated into Latvian Volunteer Police Regiment 3.

Latvian Police Front Battalion 319 was formed in Riga on 25 October 1943. Attached to Security Regiment 773 within Police Battle Group "Jeckeln", until 15 November 1943 it took part in "Operation Heinrich".[19] It was subsequently employed in the Indra area (approx. 60 km E of Dvinsk) and at the beginning of January 1944 saw action at the front with VIII Army Corps (16th Army). In March 1944 the battalion was deployed to Orlai (approx. 30 km SW of Riga) and in April 1944 was ordered to Gulbene (approx. 170 km NE of Riga). In September of that it again saw action at the front attached to the 215th Infantry Division (16th Army), and at the end of October the battalion was attached to Group "Mellenthin" (remnants of the 205th Infantry Division). It saw action with the VI SS Waffen Army Corps (Latvian) until the end of the war.

Latvian Police Battalion 320 is supposed to have been formed in Riga on 21 December 1943 and deployed in the Jelgava area, however there is no proof that the battalion was in fact established.

Latvian Police Guard Battalion 321 (Military Postal Number 10 865) was formed in Dvinsk on 21 December 1943 and stationed in the Abrene area (approx. 100 km SW of Pskov). On 14 February 1944 it was attached to Latvian Volunteer Police Regiment 3.

Latvian Police Front Battalion 322 was formed in Riga and Bauska on 23 July 1944 and on 1 August was attached to the 215th

---

19 *Ost-Pionier-Bataillon 672 (lettisches)* was deployed just to the north of it.

Areas of operations of the Latvian *Schutzmannschafts* battalions in the summer of 1943.

Infantry Division for action at the front. At the end of October 1944 the battalion was ordered to the newly-formed Army Group "Kleffel" and attached to Group "Mellenthin" (remnants of the 205th Infantry Division), part of VI SS Waffen Army Corps (Latvian). In March 1945 the battalion was attached to the 19th SS Waffen-Grenadier Division.

Latgalian *Schutzmannschafts* Battalion 325 (Military Postal Number 11 823) was formed in Riga using Latgalian manpower in March 1944. In July 1944 the battalion was handed over to the army as Construction Pioneer Battalion 325 (Latgalian) and finally, on 19 September 1944, was disbanded.

Latgalian *Schutzmannschafts* Battalion 326 (Military Postal Number 19 208) was formed in Riga in March 1944, also using Latgalian personnel, and in May it was handed over to the army as Construction Battalion 326 (Latgalian). On 1 March 1945 the remnants of the battalion were designated the 5th (Latgalian) Company and attached to Construction Pioneer Battalion 141.

Latgalian *Schutzmannschafts* Battalion 327 (Military Postal Number 03 396) was formed in Riga in March 1944 using Latgalian manpower. In May 1944 the battalion was handed over to the army as Construction Pioneer Battalion 327 (Latgalian) and was later disbanded as the army's Latgalian Construction Battalion IV.[20]

Latgalian *Schutzmannschafts* Battalion 328 (Military Postal Number 22 980) was formed in Riga in March 1944 using Latgalian personnel together with Battalions 325 to 327. In July 1944 the battalion was handed over to the army as Construction Pioneer Battalion 328 (Latgalian) and on 19 September was disbanded.

The Latvian Volunteer Police Regiments

Several administrative changes took place within the *Ordnungspolizei* in February 1943. The police regiments created by combining German police battalions in the summer of 1942 were given the affix "SS" (for example SS Police Regiment 24). In addition, new police regiments were formed which consisted of a German police battalion and two Ukrainian *Schutzmannschafts* battalions, which were often rated as rather unreliable. In a speech to *SS-Gruppenführer* in Posen on 4 October 1943, Himmler declared:

> "Now briefly to the duties of the Ordnungs- and *Sicherheitspolizei*. They have remained basically unchanged. I can only say that was has

---

20 It is likely that the original Latgalian *Schutzmannschafts* Battalions 314 and 328 were designated Latgalian Construction Battalions I-V in the army.

been achieved is enormous. We have formed about 30 police regiments from police reservists and older police soldiers—police officials, as they were formerly called. The average age in our police battalions is no worse than that in the *Wehrmacht*'s security battalions. Their performance is beyond all praise. We have also formed police rifle regiments by combining the previously- formed *Schutzmannschafts* battalions of the "wild people". No longer, therefore, are we leaving these *Schutzmannschafts* battalions alone, instead we have achieved a ratio of approximately 1 : 3. In this period of crisis we therefore have much greater stability than that which the other native or indigenous units can display."

In the spring of 1943 there were also changes for the Baltic States and their *Schutzmannschafts* battalions, which had not been characterized as "wild people" by Himmler. Three regiments were to be formed from a total of twelve *Schutzmannschafts* battalions. In honor of their service, and also as a political gesture, they would receive the designation "Police" in contrast to units from other Soviet republics.

Latvian Volunteer Police Regiment 1 was formed in Riga on 27 July 1943 from Latvian Police Battalions 277, 278, 312 and 276, initially as Police Regiment "Riga", and in September it was moved into the Dvinsk area. At the end of October the regiment took part in "Operation Heinrich" between Nevel and the Latvian border. Deployed as part of Police Battle Group "Jeckeln", it remained in the area until March 1944. The unit then returned to Latvia to rest and reequip and was renamed Latvian Volunteer Police Regiment 1. In May 1944 the regiment was moved into the Vilnius area (Lithuania) for anti-partisan operations. On 4 July 1944 it was again attached to Police Battle Group "Jeckeln", which as part of II Army Corps (16th Army) was supposed to close the gap to the 3rd Panzer Army of Army Group Center. Battle Group "Jeckeln" consisted of:

> Battle Group "Krukenberg" with Latvian Volunteer Police Regiment 3
> Battle Group "Krappe" with Latvian Border Defense Regiments 2, 4 and 6
> Battle Group "Osis"[21] with Latvian Volunteer Police Regiments 1 and 2

In mid-August 1944 the regiment was transferred to II Army Corps, part of the 18th Army, in the area southwest of Pskov. There the defending forces successfully held off the Soviets in the border

---

21 Commander of the *Ordnungspolizei* in Latvia, *Oberstleutnant* Roberts Osis (born on 18 September 1900, died 9 April 1973).

Areas of operations of the Latvian *Schutzmannschafts* and police battalions and the Latvian Volunteer Police and SS Border Defense Regiments in the summer of 1944.

region between Estonia and Russia. At the end of September 1944 the defending forces moved into the Segewold Position and the regiment was taken out of action and its remnants evacuated to Germany. On 19 November 1944 it was disbanded. The majority of the Latvians had deserted before being shipped out, and those that remained formed Construction Battalion I in the Latvian Field Replacement Depot.

Military Postal Numbers:	Headquarters	33 035
	I Battalion	38 741
	II Battalion	37 663
	III Battalion	35 182
	IV Battalion	34 909

Latvian Volunteer Police Regiment 2 (Military Postal Number 01 873) was formed in Libau in February 1944 from Latvian Police Front Battalions 22, 25, 312 and 316 and initially took part in actions against partisans in the Dvinsk area. In July 1944 it was part of Battle Group "Osis", which operated within Police Battle Group "Jeckeln". At the end of September 1944 it was transferred to SS Training Camp "Seelager" near Dundaga. What was left of the regiment was shipped to Germany and disbanded on 26 October 1944. Its remaining personnel formed Construction Battalion II in the Latvian Field Replacement Depot.

Latvian Volunteer Police Regiment 3 (Military Postal Number 08 807) was formed in Cesis (German Wenden) in February 1944 from Latvian Police Battalions 317, 318 and 321. As Army Group North's right wing was almost uncovered, *Generalmajor* Geiger (OKH Pioneer Special Staff) established a defensive position along the Dvina River using troops of the *Wehrmacht* Commander *"Ostland"*. Latvian Volunteer Police Regiment 3 was ordered into the position, along with Latvian Border Defense Regiment 5 and Security Regiment 605 (Security Battalions 210 and 1901[22]). On 4 July 1944 the regiment was attached to Battle Group "Krukenberg" (Police Battle Group "Jeckeln") and in mid-August 1944 was transferred to the 18th Army. After successful defensive fighting in the Latvian-Russian border region, the regiment was taken out of action when the Segewold Position was occupied. What was left of the regiment was evacuated to Germany and sent to the Latvian Field Replacement Depot.

The Latvian SS-Grenzschutz (Border Defense) Regiments

In the course of its winter offensive, the Red Army neared the "Panther Position", which ran from the Baltic through Narva then along Lake Peipus and the Velikaya River into the area north of Nevel. In response, hurried preparations were made for general mobilization in the Baltic States. The officer responsible was *SS-Obergruppenführer* and General der Waffen-SS Jeckeln, the Senior SS and Police Commander "Ostland and Russia North". At the end of January 1944 he held discussions

---

[22] The battalion was created by renaming Security Battalion Latvia and was later made part of the 14th Field Division (L) as II Battalion, Jäger Regiment 28 (L).

with Oskar Dankers, director of the Latvian self-government, and *SS-Brigadeführer* und *Generalmajor* der Waffen-SS Bangerskis, Inspector General of the Latvian SS Volunteer Legion. General mobilization was declared on 30 January 1944 and medical examinations of men not already called up were begun. Four days later Jeckeln announced the formation of six SS Border Defense Regiments. Although their titles included the "SS" affix, army ranks were used. Initial motivation disappeared through disorganization, shortages of equipment and arms, and inadequate training. A total of 12,118 Latvians were called up by 1 July 1944. They ultimately served in five SS Border Defense Regiments with a total of 19 battalions. The average strength of a battalion was about 650 men (four companies of 150 men each plus a headquarters).

Latvian SS Border Defense Regiment 1 was formed in Riga by orders issued on 7 February 1944 and consisted of:

Headquarters	Military Postal Number	00 850
I Battalion	Military Postal Number	02 324
II Battalion	Military Postal Number	04 554
III Battalion	Military Postal Number	06 995
IV Battalion	Military Postal Number	08 376

The regiment was disbanded in March 1944.

Latvian SS Border Defense Regiment 2 was formed in Riga by orders issued on 7 February 1944 and consisted of:

Headquarters	Military Postal Number	01 809
I Battalion	Military Postal Number	03 792
II Battalion	Military Postal Number	05 479
III Battalion	Military Postal Number	07 032
IV Battalion	Military Postal Number	09 560

At the beginning of July 1944 it was attached to Battle Group "Knappe" within Police Battle Group "Jeckeln". As part of the II Army Corps (16th Army) the regiment was supposed to restore contact with the 3rd Panzer Army (Army Group Center) in the area south of Dvinsk. In fact, however, it only succeeded in advancing as far as Widze, where a battle group of the 215th Infantry Division had been encircled. Battle Group "Jeckeln" remained in the area until 13 August 1944, when it was moved north to the II Army Corps (18th Army). There the army corps was thrown into a gap between the XXVIII and XXXVIII Army Corps created by the Soviet offensive. As part of Battle Group "Jeckeln", Latvian SS Border Defense Regiment 2 joined the neighboring XXXVIII Army Corps, which was engaged in fierce defensive fighting in the immediate border region with Estonia and Russia. On 15 August Jeckeln also took over command of the

Zanis Zvejnieks was called up in Tuckum on 16/02/1944 during the formation of Latvian Border Defense Regiment 4. On 26/08/1944 he was transferred to the mortar platoon of Latvian SS Border Defense Regiment 5.

remnants of the battered 21st Field Division (L). On 27 August 1944 he was awarded the Knight's Cross of the Iron Cross for stabilizing the front in this sector. After the 18th Army occupied the Segewold Position at the end of September 1944, Police Battle Group "Jeckeln" was taken out of action and broken up. The same applied to Latvian SS Border Defense Regiment 2, whose remnants were employed in the formation of SS Waffen Grenadier Regiment 106 (Latvian No. 7).

Latvian SS Border Defense Regiment 3 was formed in Riga by orders issued on 7 February 1944 and consisted of:

Headquarters	Military Postal Number	08 830
I Battalion	Military Postal Number	10 005
II Battalion	Military Postal Number	12 252
III Battalion	Military Postal Number	14 988
IV Battalion	Military Postal Number	00 474

To date nothing is known about its operational use. The regiment was struck from the military postal number summary and was probably disbanded after a few weeks of existence due to equipment shortages.

Latvian SS Border Defense Regiment 4 was formed in Tukkum by orders issued on 7 February 1944 and consisted of:

Headquarters	Military Postal Number	09 093
I Battalion	Military Postal Number	11 531
II Battalion	Military Postal Number	13 659
III Battalion	Military Postal Number	15 187
IV Battalion	Military Postal Number	01 267

In July 1944 it became part of Battle Group "Knapp" within Police Battle Group "Jeckeln" (see Latvian SS Border Defense Regiment 2). After seeing some action, at the end of September the regiment was disbanded and its remaining personnel were sent to Latvian SS Border Defense Regiment 5.

Latvian SS Border Defense Regiment 5 was formed in Aizpute by orders issued on 7 February 1944 and consisted of:

Headquarters	Military Postal Number	02 051[23]
I Battalion	Military Postal Number	04 573
II Battalion	Military Postal Number	06 180
III Battalion	Military Postal Number	08 361
IV Battalion	Military Postal Number	10 642

---

23 On 22 December 1944 this postal number was allocated to the Latvian Police Construction Battalion "Zvaigsne".

When the Red Army was able to break through at the seam between Army Groups North and Center, *Generalmajor* Geiger (OKH Pioneer Special Staff) established a defense position along the Dvina River using forces of the *Wehrmacht* commander *"Ostland"*. Latvian SS Border Defense Regiment 5 was ordered to man this position along with Latvian Volunteer Police Regiment 3 and Security Regiment 605. When the German military took over the line the regiment was pulled out of action and bolstered by the remnants of Latvian SS Border Defense Regiment 4. Reorganization into SS Waffen Grenadier Regiment 106 (Latvian No. 7)[24] began in October 1944.

Latvian SS Border Defense Regiment 6 was formed in Kuldiga (German Goldingen) by orders issued on 7 February 1944 and consisted of:

Headquarters	Military Postal Number	03 550
I Battalion	Military Postal Number	05 498
II Battalion	Military Postal Number	11 240
III Battalion	Military Postal Number	07 322
IV Battalion	Military Postal Number	09 761

The II Battalion was disbanded in March 1944, leaving the regiment with three battalions. In July 1944 it was part of Battle Group "Knapp" (see Latvian SS Border Defense Regiment 2) and at the end of September it was disbanded. The regiment's remaining personnel joined the Latvian Field Replacement Depot in Danzig.

Sicherheitspolizei

During the Second World War the responsibilities of the *Sicherheitspolizei*, or Security Police, included criminal police law, passport matters, immigration and emigration, and "Jewish matters". In the course of the latter range of duties, the Security Police and the SD[25] formed four *Einsatzgruppen*.

With respect to operations in eastern Europe, on 28 April 1941 Generalfeldmarschall von Brauchitsch, commander-in-chief of the Army, announced that the Sipo and SD *Einsatzgruppen* would carry out their duties[26] in the rear on their own authority and according to

---

24 This was directly attached to the VI SS Waffen Army Corps (Latvian).
25 The abbreviations Sipo and SD stood for *Sicherheitspolizei* (Security Police) and *Sicherheitsdienst* (Security Service) respectively.
26 One of its main tasks was the organized capture and concentration of the Jewish population in ghettoes, to provide direct and quick access for further actions.
In the summer of 1941 a systematic eradication was not feasible because of the low strengths of the *Einsatzgruppen* and their respective *Einsatzkommando*s. The first mass shootings, including in Latvia, were carried out by radical anti-Semitic groups, sometimes without the knowledge of the German authorities.

the directives issued by *SS-Obergruppenführer* Heydrich, head of the Sipo and SD.

Of the battalion-strength *Einsatzgruppen* (A-D), *Einsatzgruppe* "A" under *SS-Brigadeführer* Stahlecker[27] operated in the Baltic States. It was organized into four company-strength *Einsatzkommando*s (1a, 1b, 2 and 3), of which *Einsatzkommando* 2 operated in Latvia.

The leader of *Einsatzkommando* 2, SS-Sturmbannführer Dr. Lange[28], who from December 1941 was also commander of the Security Police and SD in Latvia with headquarters in Riga, initially had about 170 men under his command. As this was insufficient to carry out the *Einsatzkommando*'s assigned tasks, which were the result of Berlin's demands for mass executions, Dr. Lange recruited local volunteers as so-called "auxiliary police" or "auxiliary security-police to assist. *SS-Strumbannführer* Victor Arajs[29] became well known after the war. With as many as 500 Latvian volunteers, he took part

---

When the ultimate directive arrived from Berlin as to how the Jews (in the Baltic) were to be treated and for the most part liquidated, the *Einsatzgruppen* and *Einsatzkommando*s fell back on these known extremists.

27 Stahlecker became commander of the Sipo and SD in the Reich Commissariat "Ostland".

28 Dr. Rudolf Lange was born in Weißwasser on 18 April 1910. After attending law school, in 1936 he joined the SS and worked with the Gestapo in Berlin. When *Einsatzgruppe* A was formed he functioned as Department Head IV (Gestapo) and V (Kripo) and was supposed to work with the appropriate Latvian police authorities and organize them on the German model. In October 1941 he had a camp set up for German Jews in Salaspils and oversaw the liquidation of Latvian Jews in order to make room in the ghetto for the flow of German Jews being deported to Latvia. Most of the shootings were carried out by the Latvian Arajs Commando. Lange attended the Wannsee Conference in January 1942 and in January 1945 was appointed commander of the Sipo and SD in the Wartheland in Posen. Promoted to *SS-Standartenführer*, on 6 February 1945 Dr. Rudolf
Lange was awarded the German Cross in Gold for the defense of the city. He was seriously wounded and committed suicide in Fortress Posen on 23 February 1945.

29 Victors Arajs was born in Baldone (Latvia) on 13 January 1910. After graduating from school he served in the Latvian Army and later became a lieutenant in the Latvian Police. Taken into German service, in 1943 he was appointed *SS-Sturmbannführer* and *Major der Ordnungspolizei*. Toward the end of the war he became a battalion commander in the 15th SS Waffen Grenadier Regiment (Latvian No.1) with the rank of *Waffen-Sturmbannführer*. On 2 March 1945, for failing to obey the orders of the commander of SS Waffen Grenadier Regiment 34 (Latvian No.5), he was transferred to the division's officer reserve. After the war he initially lived in Delmenhorst under a false name and later in Frankfurt/Main. When his true identity was discovered, Arajs was tried and found guilty by the district court in Hamburg of executing Jews in the Rumbula Forest. Sentenced to life imprisonment, he died in the Karlsruhe penal institution in 1988.

In October 1941 the Security Police set up a camp in Salaspils, which initially housed mainly Latvian and German Jews employed to cut peat. Later it was used to hold political prisoners (mainly Latvians) and so-called "suspected partisans" captured in anti-partisan operations. On average the camp housed about 2,000 inmates—altogether about 12,000 people passed through the "Kurtenhof expanded police prison and work/reeducation camp" (Salaspils).

in the mass shooting of Latvian Jews and an as deported to Latvia.[30] The Latvian volunteers were recruited by Gustavs Celmins, head of the Thunder Cross organization[31]. Earlier, on 4 July 1941, he had published a call for a war against the "harmful elements"[32] in Latvian in the nationalist newspaper *Tevija* (Fatherland):

> "To all national-thinking Latvians, Thunder Cross members, students, officers, defense troops and citizens who are ready to take an active part in ridding our country of harmful elements."

In a letter to the General Commissioner "Latvia" Drechsler dated 11 October 1941, Dr. Walter Alnor, administrator of the district of Eckernförde and later regional commissar in Latvian Libau, described the unbelievable actions against the Jewish population and the behavior of the Latvian auxiliary police:

> "A disquieting incident was the resumption of shootings of large numbers of Jews in the past week. All of the Jews have been liquidated in the rural areas and small towns, and approximately 470 in Libau itself. Almost all were women and children. In Hasenpoth, for example, there were just twelve male Jews left and 321 women and children. These were all shot. The fortress commander and I both voiced our opposition to the fact that, after weeks of complete quiet, such shootings, which are also contrary to the orders of the Reich

---

30 In particular, these included the executions in the Riga ghetto and the Rumbula Forest on 30 November and 8 December 1941. Hitler had given the order for the deportation of German Jews to the east in September 1941. When the original destination of Minsk became unable to accept any more forced evacuees, the trains were rerouted to Riga. The Riga ghetto soon became overcrowded, and on 30 November 1941 1,053 Jews from Berlin on one of the first trains were liquidated in Rumbula Forest. The next four trains to arrive carried about 4,000 persons. By order of *SS-Brigadeführer* Stahlecker they were housed on an empty farm, which later became a concentration camp called Jungfernhof. On 30 November 1941 the Riga ghetto was also "cleared" to make room for more transports of German Jews. In the process approximately 15,000 Latvian Jews were presumably killed, as well as another 12,500 Jews in Rumbula on 8 and 9 December.
31 The extremely nationalist-oriented movement, which called itself "Thunder Cross" (*Perkonskrusts* in Latvian) and had about 10,000 registered members, had been banned by the Latvian government in 1933. In 1941 it hoped to achieve political power with the help of the Germans. For various reasons, however, Hitler had little interest. He did, however, authorize the use of its members, previously organized into battle groups, in the *Ordnungs- and Sicherheitspolizei*.
32 "Harmful elements" referred primarily to Jews and communists.

The life story of *Waffen-Sturmbannführer* Konstantins Mucenieks. Initially a member of the Security Police, in June 1944 he was attached to the headquarters staff of the Latvian SS Volunteer Division and on 22 November 1944 was transferred to the headquarters staff of SS Waffen Grenadier Regiment 32 (Latvian No.5):

"I was born in Riga on 16 December 1903, the oldest son of the civil servant Adams Mucenieks and his wife Lena. I spent my childhood in Riga. During the World War the families of civil servants were evacuated and my family was sent to the interior of Russia. There I attended high school in Novgorod. After the Russian Revolution broke out, in 1918 we returned to Latvia. Afterwards I lived exclusively in Riga. My mother died in 1920, my father in 1923, while I was still attending school. I was therefore compelled to work during my last year of school. I found a job with the railroad administration. After finishing school, in the autumn of 1924 I entered the Latvian officer school. I graduated at the top of my class in 1927. Following promotion to lieutenant, I was assigned to the Latvian Army's 8th Dvinsk Infantry Regiment. I served in the 8th Regiment until 1933. In July of that year I was transferred to the 5th Wenden Infantry Regiment. During that time I was twice seconded to the Pioneer Regiment to take pioneer classes. I completed the course very successfully and in 1936 I qualified as a pioneer officer. After passing the necessary test, in 1937 I was accepted into the military academy. On 29 December 1939 I graduated from the academy. On 11 November of that year, while still at the military academy, I was transferred from the 5th Infantry Regiment to the training department in the army headquarters staff and appointed assistant to a section leader. On 10 May 1940 I was promoted to captain with an effective date of 1 September 1932. During the summer of 1940 I was attached to the officer school as a group leader to train new officers. When the course ended I returned to the headquarters staff. When the Latvian Army was subsequently incorporated into the Red Army, I was discharged as unsuitable for the Red Army, in large part due to my own efforts. In this way I escaped the humiliation of having to serve in this army. I subsequently obtained a modest position in the Riga city administration and was initially employed as a technician and later as an accountant in the city's building and property management department. I held this position during the entire Bolshevik period. Once, in the spring of 1941, I was summoned by the war commissariat of the city of Riga. There, I and all the officers who had left the service were offered the well-paid position of a leader of pre-military student training. I declined, despite the salary difference. After the wave of arrests in June 1941, I stayed with relatives in Riga Beach without registering. From 1 July 1941 I was active in the Latvian Self-Defense. When the self-defense force ceased its activities, on 17 July I volunteered for service with the German military, however the military administration headquarters in Riga assigned me to the security police, where I was taken on as an interpreter on 25 July. I stayed in the German security police until 5 June 1943, when I asked for my release so that I could volunteer for the Latvian SS Legion. On 5 June 1943 I joined the Latvian SS Volunteer Division with the rank of *Hauptsturmführer*."

On 26 June 1944, *SS-Oberführer* Heilmann, commander of the 15th SS Waffen Grenadier Division (Latvian No.1), wrote an evaluation of the then *Waffen-Hauptsturmführer*:

"Sound character, quiet demeanor, prefers not to stand out. Good mental disposition, slim in appearance. M., who formerly successfully attended the Latvian military academy, was previously employed as a Latvian aide-de-camp in the tactical section of the operations group. He functioned as an interpreter and performed aide-de-camp duties. He carried out his tasks satisfactorily. He possesses useful tactical knowledge. His behavior toward superiors has been impeccable, and he has the ability to be convincing. M. is a committed anti-Bolshevik and is also very concerned about Latvian prestige and interests. At present M. is attending a battalion commander's course. It is intended that he should be appointed commander of III Battalion, SS Waffen Grenadier Regiment 34."

commissar, were carried out.[33] The shooting of women and children, some of whom were led crying to the places of execution, has caused general dismay. The completely submissive mayor of the city of Libau, who, under constant pressure from the various *Wehrmacht* elements, approved almost every measure, approached me personally and referred to the great uproar in the city. Military officers have also asked me if this gruesome manner of execution, even against children, is necessary. In every civilized state the killing of pregnant women is forbidden, as it was even during the Middle Ages. Here they have taken no account of this. The fortress commander of Windau told me that four Latvian self-defense people showed up, two of whom were totally drunk, in order to, as they proclaimed loudly in the street, "carry out the liquidation of the Jews". The local commander later received instructions not to interfere with the activities of these elements. I am convinced that one day this will prove to be a serious mistake. That is unless all of the elements involved are also subsequently liquidated."

In addition to the executions from the summer of 1941 to spring of 1942, Sonderkommando Arajs also took part in actions in and outside Latvia until the summer of 1944. It was attached to the Senior SS and Police Commander "Ostland and Russia North" for operations against the partisans, which also included the killing of Jews. In the summer of 1944 the bulk of the Kommando, including its commander, was incorporated into the 15th SS Waffen Grenadier Division (Latvian No.1).

LATVIAN SS VOLUNTEER LEGION

With approximately 8,000 Latvian volunteers already serving in the *Schutzmannschafts* battalions of the *Ordnungspolizei*, after the tragedy at Stalingrad Hitler authorized the formation of large military units in Latvia.[34] Because of the country's racial background, the recruiting was done by the Waffen-SS. It was hoped that this would allow 50,000 Latvians to be quickly recruited for military service. On 10 February 1943 issued the following order to SS Headquarters:

---

33 Reich Commissar Lohse temporarily put a halt to such killings. Dr. Leibbrandt, department head in the "State Ministry for the Occupied Eastern Territories" in Berlin, subsequently requested an explanation: *"The Reich Central Security Office has complained that the Reich Commissar Ostland has prohibited the shooting of Jews in Libau. I am requesting an immediate report on the matter in question."* One can see that not all of the functionaries of the Third Reich who became involved with Jewish policies advocated the same radical solution, though in the end they resigned themselves to it.

34 In principle, Hitler had so far only authorized the formation of security units no larger than battalion size. In addition to fears that larger formations might pose a security risk, the refusal was also caused by reluctance to deal with the related political demands by the respective foreign politicians.

Induction notice from spring 1943: "Enlistment in the SS Legion".

"I order the formation of a Latvian SS volunteer legion. The size and type of the unit will depend on the number of Latvian men available."

An initial intake of men affected those from the 1919 to 1924 age classes subject to compulsory labor service, who were given the option of serving in the military instead. Of the approximately 70,000 young Latvians who were mustered, 30,000 volunteered for the Latvian SS Volunteer

Legion. Himmler's expectations of 50,000 volunteers were thus not met. Nevertheless, on 26 February 1943 orders were issued for the formation of a Latvian SS Volunteer Division of about 18,000 men, and on 11 March 1943 the order was given to reorganize the 2nd SS Motorized Infantry Brigade into the Latvian SS Volunteer Brigade with about 8,000 men.

In contrast to most battalion-strength volunteer legions from Western Europe (such as the Volunteer Legion *"Flandern"*), the formulation *"Latvian SS Volunteer Legion"* did not characterize a formation per se, but instead was a collective designation for all Latvian SS volunteers sent from there to other units. This included those who, primarily on account of their limited suitability, were transferred to the *SS-Wachsturmbannen* (guard battalions) in concentration and labor camps. It may be assumed that about 2,000 Latvians served in these units, at least for a time. Former *SS-Hauptscharführer* Heinz Müller recalled:

> "I was born in Saxony on 25 November 1923 and in 1941 was conscripted into the SS-Totenkopf-Division. After I was badly wounded at Kursk in the summer of 1943 (head wound resulting in blindness in my left eye and a penetrating bullet wound in the back) and spending a year in hospital, on 6 July 1944 I was transferred to Sachsenhausen concentration camp. While the Latvians and Ukrainians were housed in the camp itself, we were quartered outside the grounds. As an *SS-Hauptscharführer*, I was often a sentry commander on the concentration camp's main tower. Between three and six men were stationed there as a rule. The tower was armed with rifles and one or two machine-guns. A light machine-gun was posted in each of the other towers.
>
> The Latvian guards were addressed as Waffen-Grenadiers and wore field-gray uniforms. On the other hand the Ukrainians, or so-called Travniki Men as they were called, wore brown uniforms with black forage caps. Relations with the foreign personnel were so so, though they tended to abuse alcohol on a regular basis. There were several Baltic Germans among the Latvians, for they sometimes spoke German to us.
>
> Assaults against concentration camp inmates by German guards were uncommon, however the Ukrainians in particular frequently beat them for absolutely no reason.
>
> After the attempt on Hitler's life, Hitler's speech was broadcast over the camp loudspeaker. We were then given questionnaires about persons and irregularities.
>
> On 2 March 1945 I was transferred to Prague and my tour at Sachsenhausen concentration camp came to an end. On 9 May 1945 I was captured by the Soviets in Prague and was subsequently held as a prisoner of war for six years."

A second wave of draft registrations in October 1943 (age classes 1919 to 1924 and 1912 to 1918) resulted in approximately 5,000 more

Latvians being drafted into the Waffen-SS. Just one moth later the 1925 age class was called up, and on 21 December 1943 the SS-FHA (SS Operational Headquarters) ordered the formation of Latvian SS Volunteer Grenadier Training and Replacement Brigade 15 in Mitau for these numerous recruits. Teofils Dreimanis was called up in autumn 1943. He recalled his service in the Waffen-SS:

> "I was born in Cesis in 1917 and served in the Latvian Army in 1939-40. Following the introduction of compulsory labor service, in the autumn of 1943 I registered for the draft and decided on military service. I initially earned my driver's permit for fully-tracked vehicles up to 40 tons and motorcycles and then worked for a short time as a driving instructor for other recruits. Then in the spring of 1944 I was transferred to SS Flak Battalion 19. My commanding officer was *Legions-Obersturmbannführer* Harris Gusevs, who in the summer of 1944 also commanded SS Flak Battalion 106, which was formed by combining the flak battalions of the two Latvian SS divisions. Assigned to 88-mm anti-aircraft guns, I took part in the retreat to the Velikaya and then the fighting in the homeland. I was captured by the Soviets in Sabile (Courland). They relieved me of my wristwatch and my boots. For my service in the Waffen-SS I was forced to work in a gulag in Karelia until 1959."

In January 1944, with general mobilization imminent, an order was issued for the 2nd Latvian SS Volunteer Brigade to be expanded into the 19th Latvian SS Volunteer Division. Thus two grenadier divisions were formed. After the collapse of the front in 1944 and the evacuation of numerous remnants of police and SS border defense regiments to Germany, a Latvian Field Replacement Depot was also set up, which numbered more than 10,000 men. Although there was a close association with the Waffen-SS – for example the commanding officer was a member of the Waffen-SS – this was not indicated by the unit designation. In planning, at least, the Latvian Field Replacement Depot had the organization of an Infantry Division 44 and thus in purely numerical terms formed a third Latvian division.

THE 15TH SS WAFFEN GRENADIER DIVISION (LATVIAN NO.1)

On 10 February 1943 Hitler ordered the formation of a Latvian SS volunteer legion. After discussions with former Latvian General Bangerskis, who had been named inspector of the Latvian SS Volunteer Legion, Himmler issued guidelines for the drafting of Latvian men. The minimum height for police volunteers was set at 1.64 meters, and 1.68 meters for the Waffen-SS. The Latvian government (Directorate

Teofils Dreimanis as a Kapralis in the Latvian Army in 1939 and in 1943 as a *Legions-Unterscharführer*. He functioned as a driving instructor for members of the Latvian SS Volunteer Legion. For the most part, however, only the corps units of the VI SS Volunteer Army Corps (Latvian) were motorized. Below: Heavy prime movers (Sd.Kfz.9) of SS Corps Artillery Battalion 106.

General for Defense) was to be responsible for drafting and examining prospective personnel. An SS recruiting detachment was also set up in Riga. It ultimately became SS Recruiting Detachment *"Ostland"* and operated under the command of *SS-Standartenführer* Hierthes.

After the approximate number of volunteers was determined, on 15 February 1943 Hitler issued the formation order for a Latvian SS Volunteer Legion. The unit, which was authorized to use Latvian as its language of command and whose members used Waffen-SS ranks with the prefix *"Legions"*[35], was supposed to be established as an infantry division in the Reich Commissariat of *"Ostland"*. The units were quartered as follows:

Division Headquarters	Riga
SS Volunteer Regiment 1 (I-III Battalions)	Paplaka/Libau
SS Volunteer Regiment 2 (ditto)	Vainode
SS Volunteer Regiment 3 (ditto)	Wenden
SS Volunteer Artillery Regiment (I-IV Battalions)	Mitau
SS Anti-Tank Battalion	Grobinau
SS Pioneer Battalion	Mitau
SS Signals Battalion	Tukkum
SS Field Replacement Battalion	Cekule
SS Flak Battalion	Grobina
SS Fusilier Battalion	Windau

For lack of a suitable division commander, *SS-Brigadeführer* Hansen, the inspector of artillery and flak in SS Operational Headquarters was initially named commander of the formation staff. After about ten weeks he transferred command to *SS-Brigadeführer* Pückler-Burghaus, the former commander of the Waffen-SS in the Protectorate of Bohemia-Moravia. Something new was the appointment of an infantry leader, who received his orders from the division commander but was explicitly responsible for employment of the infantry. In order to make the Latvian grenadiers feel that they were under the command of one of their countrymen, on 1 March 1943 Arturs Silgailis[36] was given the rank of *Legions-Standartenführer* and named infantry leader of the Latvian SS Volunteer Division.

---

35 For example *Legions-Rottenführer* or *Legions-Hauptsturmführer*.
36 Arturs Silgailis was born in Mezmuiza (Latvia) on 13 November 1895 and in 1914 entered the Russian Army's officer school. He received his commission as a lieutenant on 13 September 1915. After serving in the army he joined the Baltic Fleet. When the Latvian SS Volunteer Legion was formed he became a *Legions-Standartenführer* and infantry commander. On 9 November 1943 he was promoted to *Legions-Oberführer*. On 6 July 1944 he joined the inspectorate of the Latvian SS Volunteer Legion under *SS-Gruppenführer* Bangerskis and became Chief-of-Staff. After the war he emigrated to Canada and died in Toronto at the age of 101.

The greatest difficulty during formation of the new division was providing it with uniforms, weapons and equipment. In addition to its personnel losses, the military had lost huge amounts of equipment at Stalingrad and in Africa, and in the year 1943 the German armaments industry was incapable of meeting the enormous requirements of the *Wehrmacht*, Waffen-SS and police. As a result, it proved impossible to begin equipping the new division in April 1943 as announced. Materiel shortages also hampered training of the new recruits, and consequently the division went into action without basic preparation.

At the end of September 1943 the division command received orders to transfer approximately 1,000 men to the 2nd Latvian SS Volunteer Brigade to make good losses suffered in the fighting at the Volkhov.

One month later the units of the Waffen-SS were numbered consecutively. The Latvian SS Volunteer Division was given the number "15" and the regiments the titles:

SS Volunteer Grenadier Regiment 32 (Latvian No.3)[37]
SS Volunteer Grenadier Regiment 33 (Latvian No.4)
SS Volunteer Grenadier Regiment 34 (Latvian No.5)
SS Volunteer Artillery Regiment 15 (Latvian No.1)

Operational readiness was supposed to be achieved after eight months,[38] and so at the beginning of November 1943 the 15th SS Volunteer Division (Latvian No.1) received orders to join Army Group North. Attached to the XXXXIII Army Corps, the units initially manned a second line ("Barbarossa Position") north of Nevel, which was about five kilometers behind the actual main line of resistance. The division command post was set up in Sokolniki. The grenadier companies took turns in the positions of the 83rd and 204th Infantry Divisions in order to gain some experience of the front. At the same time SS Volunteer Artillery Regiment 15 was attached to the 205th Artillery Regiment. Until 20 November elements of SS Volunteer Grenadier Regiment 34 took part in an anti-partisan action with the 281st Security Division.

On 31 December 1943 the division made the following strength report:

	Officers	NCOs	Enlisted Men	Total
Actual	471	1,330	13,391	15,192
	3.1%	8.75%	88.15%	100%
Authorized	475	2,588	11,619	14,682
	3.2%	17.6%	79.2%	100%

---

37 The two grenadier regiments of the 2nd Latvian SS Volunteer Brigade were designated "Latvian No.1 and 2".
38 Basically, an eight-month training period was considered adequate for an infantry Division.

Compulsory labor service for age classes 1919-1924 was declared in Latvia on 25 February 1943. The young men could choose to volunteer to serve in the Latvian SS Volunteer Legion.

Swearing-in ceremony with German and Latvian flags in the background.

With almost half of its non-commissioned officer positions unfilled, the division was far from fully fit for operations. At the end of January 1944, as part of X Army Corps (16th Army), the division relieved the 21st Field Division (L) south of Staraya Russa. The unit took over its own sector of the front south of Lake Ilmen. Approximately 35 km in width, it extended from Ratschi (approx. 40 km W of Kholm) to Kamenka (approx. 20 km NW of Kholm) along the Lovat River.

In the course of its winter offensive, the Red Army was able to break through at the seam between the German 18th and 16th Armies. After attempts to close the gap failed, on 18 February 1944 Army Group North ordered a withdrawal to the "Panther Position".[39] When large-scale combat operations proved too much for the division commander, the energetic *SS-Oberführer* Heilmann assumed command.

The 16th Army's withdrawal proceeded according to plan with minimal casualties. The few motorized units of the 15th SS Volunteer Division drove unchecked over the crowded road in the direction of Ostrov. The remaining units, most of whom took secondary roads through forests and marshes, were repeatedly attacked by partisans. At the end of February, after covering about 140 km, the men arrived in the "Panther Position" in the area south of Ostrov extending to Novgorodka (approx. 30 km S of Ostrov).

There it was placed under the general command of the VI SS Volunteer Army Corps (Latvian), together with the 2nd Latvian SS Volunteer Brigade and the 21st Field Division (L). Now part of the 18th Army, from their well-fortified positions in the area of the Velikaya the units attempted to stop the Red Army. On 11 March 1944 the *Wehrmacht* communiqué declared:

> "In the north of the Eastern Front the Bolsheviks attacked northwest of Nevel, in the Ostrov area, at Pskov and at Narva, supported by powerful tank and air forces. Their attempts to break through failed due to the stubborn resistance offered by troops of the army, the Waffen-SS and Latvian and Estonian volunteer units. Immediate counterattacks eliminated or sealed off local penetrations. The enemy lost 101 tanks."

On 16 March 1944 the enemy broke through at the junction between the Latvian SS division and the Latvian SS brigade., occupying Hill 93.4. A mixed Latvian battle group launched a counterattack. It consisted of:

---

39 Construction of the Panther Position was begun in September 1943. Approximately 15,000 construction pioneers, 7,500 members of the Todt Organization and more than 20,000 Russian civilians were employed in its construction. South of Lake Peipus, it extended along the Velikaya to the Tobolenets area and from there east to Lake Alje and finally south to Ivan Lake north of Nevel.

Young recruits of the Latvian SS Volunteer Division during training in the summer of 1943. Note that their collar tabs are still without SS runes or symbols (middle photo).

reinforced I Battalion, SS Volunteer Grenadier Regiment 32
SS Fusilier Battalion 15
III Battalion, SS Volunteer Grenadier Regiment 43
II Battalion, SS Volunteer Grenadier Regiment 44

The fighting was fierce and the Latvian battle group retook the hill and held it against enemy counterattacks. The *Wehrmacht* reported on the action in the German newspapers:

> "On the remaining Eastern Front the Soviets attacked in the area west of Nevel, near Ostrov and on the Narva front. Latvian SS volunteer units played a prominent part in fighting off these attacks."

On 26 March 1944 the Red Army launched another attack with the objective of breaching the "Panther Position". Enemy troops crossed the Velikaya and established a three by five kilometer bridgehead. The next day the *Wehrmacht* communiqué described the action, trivializing the drama:

> "In the area south of Ostrov, Latvian SS volunteer units, together with German troops, repulsed assaults by several enemy divisions. A local penetration was sealed off."

Attempts to eliminate the bridgehead failed, nevertheless on 29 March 1944 the newspapers reported:

> "In heavy fighting, heavy enemy attacks were repulsed by German troops and Latvian SS volunteer units southeast of Ostrov and on the Narva front."

On 10 April 1944 the Red Army temporarily halted its offensive along the Velikaya. It had achieved its objective of gaining a bridgehead. The 15th Latvian SS Volunteer Division had been badly battered in the previous battles, and Army Group North ordered it to rest and reequip in the 16th Army's area. As part of VI SS Volunteer Army Corps, the division was sent into the area northeast of Opochka, where it received replacement personnel and equipment. In June 1944 the unit was renamed the **15th SS Waffen Grenadier Division (Latvian No.1)**.

On 10 July 1944, as part of the Soviet summer offensive, the 2nd Baltic Front attacked the VI SS Volunteer Army Corps deployed on the 16th Army's left wing. The very next day the corps' tactically less than adept commanding general, *SS-Gruppenführer* Treuenfeld, ordered the units withdrawn toward the so-called "Odenwald Position"[40]. Instead

---

40 It followed a line Alolya River-Berezovskoye Lake-Zubovo-Shegino-Lyebedinyetza.

of meeting cohesive resistance, the Soviet troops encountered a front in motion. Powerful enemy armored forces drove into the retreat, resulting in chaos. By 12 July 1944 the Latvian army corps was already nearing Opochka and the next day it crossed the Velikaya, some of the troops by swimming. The corps abandoned most of its heavy weapons and equipment. Contact with its neighbor on the left, the L Army Corps (18th Army) to the north, was lost. Though some companies fought bravely, the 15th SS Waffen Grenadier Division lost cohesion.

It was obvious that the officers, from the commanding general to the regimental commanders, had been over their heads. Treuenfeld was summoned to the army group headquarters in Rositten to answer for his failure. Because of the chaotic retreat by the VI SS Waffen Army Corps (Latvian), the 23rd and 93rd Infantry Divisions were also nearly destroyed. Himmler had Treuenfeld and *SS-Oberführer* Heilmann, commander of the 15th SS Waffen Grenadier Division, immediately relieved. The latter had recently had a number of Latvians shot for losing their weapons and equipment during the retreat. The situation threatened to escalate completely! Hundreds of Latvians left their units and tried to make their way to the west on their own.

The remnants of the 15th SS Waffen Grenadier Division (Latvian No.1) were initially attached to the 23rd Infantry Division and moved into defense lines. When the Red Army broke through the front between Sebesh and Opochka on 15 June, the units received orders to retreat to avoid being cut off. The next day they crossed the Issa near Kozenec. SS Battle Group Aperats, formed from the remnants of SS Waffen-Grenadier Regiments 32 and 33 and elements of Grenadier Regiment 159, was

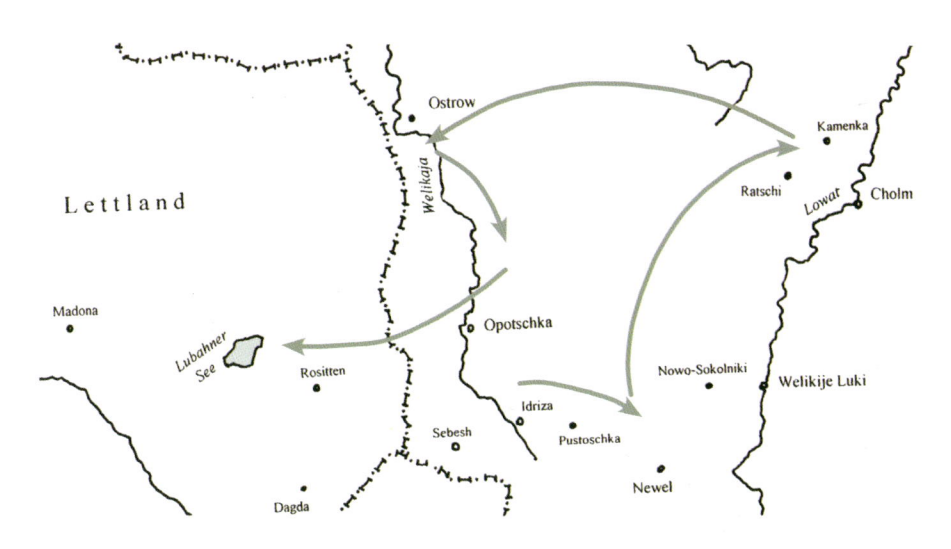

The path of the 15th SS Volunteer Division from October 1943 to July 1944.

Officers of the 15th SS Waffen
Grenadier Division (Latvian No.1).

Abschrift.

SS-Führungshauptamt
Amt V /IIa Ref. 6
Az: 21a13.Ku/Br.

Berlin-Wilmersdorf, den 2.12.1943.

Betr.: Übernahme und Einstufung ehem. lett. Offiziere.
Anlg.: - 17 -

An das
SS-Personalhauptamt.

In der Anlage überreicht das SS-Führungshauptamt, Amt. IIa, Übernahmeanträge für 17 ehem. Offiziere der lett. Wehrmacht, die sich z.Zt. bei der lett. SS-Freiw.-Brigade befinden.

Es wird gebeten, dieselben mit dem angegebenen Dienstgrad in die Waffen-SS zu übernehmen und einzustufen.

Sämtliche Offiziere waren vor ihrer Einstellung in die SS-Frw.-Brigade bei den Schutzmannschafts-Btl. und haben sich dort Auszeichnungen erworben.

Die noch fehlenden Lichtbilder sind angefordert und werden nach Eingang nachgereicht.

Übernahme als Frw.-SS-Obersturmführer:

Eglitis	Ansis	13.4.09,	m.W.v.	1.4.1943,
Krasts	Paulis	6.8.06,	"	1.5.1943,
Mals	Voldemars	23.4.16	"	1.4.1943,
Konrads-Konrats	Fridrichs	20.5.06	"	1.6.1943.

Übernahme als Freiw.-SS-Untersturmführer:

Dute	Vilis	23. 7.10,	"	1. 6.1943,
Everts	Voldemars	1. 3.02	"	1. 6.1943,
Mazurs	Juris	20. 3.87,	"	1. 7.1943,
Rubenis	Karlis	3. 1.06,	"	1. 6.1943.

pp.

gez.
Dr. Katz
SS-Oberführer.

F.d.R.d.A.
SS-Oberscharführer.

SS-Personalhauptamt II W   Berlin, den 6. Juni 1944.
II W II Abt. 3
Az.: Nr.

Betr.: Beförderungen.

Sonderverteiler.

Nachstehend aufgeführte Offiziere sind befördert worden:

Zum Waffen-Hauptsturmführer mit Wirkung vom 9. 11. 1943:

Baumanis, Valdemars	geb.	19.4.05	15.Waffen-Gren.Div.-SS
Silis, Jekabs	"	23.2.04	"
Sprogis, Aleksandrs	"	18.6.06	"
Tervits, Jekabs	"	27.2.08	"

Zum Waffen-Obersturmführer mit Wirkung vom 9. 11. 1943:

Bite, Edgars	"	6.6.17	15.Waffen-Gren.Div.-SS
Janelsins, Peteris	"	26.5.16	"
Kauls, Juris	"	12.12.12	"
Kinžis, Austris	"	30.12.15	"
Lapins, Nikolajs	"	17.3.15	"
Leconis, Harijs	"	18.3.14	"
Majors, Paulis	"	23.1.02	"
Martizens, Boriss	"	13.7.13	"
Muiznieks, Janis	"	25.4.11	"
Osans, Konrad	"	15.10.10	"
Sarma, Arvids	"	27.8.11	"
Schneider, Arvids	"	10.8.03	"
Silina, Aleksandrs	"	1.9.14	"
Umile, Aleksandrs	"	18.4.02	"

Zum Waffen-Untersturmführer mit Wirkung vom 1. 12. 1943:

Apinis, Karlis	"	9.1.04	15.Waffen-Gren.Div.-SS
Berzins, Arturs	"	28.6.06	"
Brombergs, Lonids	"	31.8.13	"
Caune, Voldemars	"	7.5.01	"
Karklins, Voldemars	"	14.10.04	"
Krauja, Peters	"	27.12.14	"
Krumins, Janis	"	30.9.00	"
Purins, Arturs	"	10.11.04	"
Saulitis, Herberts	"	15.8.00	"
Sprogis, Janis	"	21.3.04	"
Userovskis, Ludvigs	"	20.12.06	"
Zauermanis, Voldemars	"	30.10.11	"
Zakis, Julijs	"	13.2.09	"

Zum Waffen-Obersturmbannführer mit Wirkung vom 30. 1. 1944:

Kozinsch, Rudolf	"	15.12.07	19.Waffen-Gren.Div.-SS

Zum Waffen-Sturmbannführer mit Wirkung vom 30. 1. 1944:

Galdinsch, Nikolajs	"	9.10.02	19.Waffen-Gren.Div.-SS
Krants, Vilis	"	17.2.05	"
Krauja, Alfons	"	4.12.99	"

- 2 -

Zum Waffen-Hauptsturmführer mit Wirkung vom 30. 1. 1944:

Bergs, Arturs	geb.	18.10.09	19.Waffen-Gren.Div.-H
Eglitis, Ansis	"	13.4.09	"
Jaunsils, Janis	"	2.3.06	"
Konrads-Kondrats, Friedrichs	"	20.5.06	"
Krasts, Paulis	"	6.8.06	"
Kvalbergs, Peteris	"	4.5.07	"
Mals, Voldemars	"	23.4.16	"

Zum Waffen-Obersturmführer mit Wirkung vom 30. 1. 1944:

Aiviekste, Miervaldis	"	2.12.17	19.Waffen-Gren.Div.-H
Bedrits, Alberts	"	14.10.02	"
Everts, Voldemars	"	1.3.02	"
Lukins, Spricis	"	31.1.00	"
Mazurs, Juris	"	20.3.07	"
Ruhenis, Karlis	"	3.1.06	"
Schnukuts, Leons	"	27.2.16	"
Spalvinsch, Peteris	"	5.5.08	"
Strautinsch, Alberts	"	29.11.15	"
Tidemanis, Eduards	"	15.8.08	"
Vilnis, Aleksanders	"	22.2.14	"
Vinklers, Olgerts	"	3.1.17	"
Ziedainis, Peteris	"	12.1.15	"

Zum Waffen-Untersturmführer mit Wirkung vom 30. 1. 1944:

Butkus, Zanis	"	29.7.06	19.Waffen-Gren.Div.-H
Diedrichsen, Georgs	"	6.6.06	"
Drubazs, Arvids	"	19.12.	"
Jakobsons, Janis	"	18.3.95	"
Krums, Zanis	"	1.12.	"
Miglans, Antons	"	22.5.02	"
Odinsch, Georgs	"	18.6.13	"
Stans, Janis	"	2.4.16	"
Tukums, Peteris	"	5.1.20	"

Zum Waffen-Standartenführer mit Wirkung vom 20. 4. 1944:

Lobe, Karlis	"	26.3.95	19.Waffen-Gren.Div.-H

Zum Waffen-Sturmbannführer mit Wirkung vom 20. 4. 1944:

Alksnitis, Augusts	"	8.11.02	15.Waffen-Gren.Div.-H
Ameriks, Alberts	"	26.12.99	"
Augstkalns, Karlis	"	11.10.04	"
Insbergs, Kristaps	"	19.12.05	"
Lapainis, Peteris	"	13.5.97	"
Lasdunieds, Jekabs	"	13.8.04	"
Melcers, Nikolai	"	13.6.98	"
Rebergs, Karlis	"	25.7.04	"
Trezins, Leonards	"	12.6.05	"
Zalitis, Arvids	"	27.2.03	"

Zum Waffen-Hauptsturmführer mit Wirkung vom 20. 4. 1944:

Eglite, Egons	"	25.7.15	15.Waffen-Gren.Div.-
Endzins, Arvids	"	6.3.15	"
Seibelis, Georgs	"	13.2.13	19.
Skurulis, Selvestrs	"	1.1.06	15.
Tute, Janis	"	20.10.05	"
Veveris, Janis-Alfreds	"	2.3.08	"

- 3 -

```
- 3 -

Zum Waffen-Obersturmführer mit Wirkung vom 20.4.1944:

Brikmanis, Arturs           geb.  4.12.11      15.Waffen-Gren.Div.
Greberga, Rudolfs            "   15.6.14             "
Kubulins, Paulis             "    1.3.14             "
Martinsons, Gustavs          "    5.8.09             "
Muncis, Hermanis             "    6.12.04            "

Zum Waffen-Untersturmführer mit Wirkung vom 20.4.1944:

Wittkus, Wladislaus-Peter    "   23.9.12      15. Waffen-Gren.Div.


                          gez. Dr. K a t z
                          SS-Brigadeführer u. Generalmajor
                               der Waffen-SS

F.d.R.
       [signature]
SS-Obersturmführer.
```

Approximately 1,400 Latvians became officers. The bulk of them had previously served in the Latvian Army and, as a rule, were taken into the Latvian SS Volunteer Legion at their previous rank. As well, four courses for Germanic officers were held at the SS officer school in Bad Tölz. About 200 Latvian *SS-Standarten*-Oberjunker passed the course.

smashed by Soviet armor south of Krassnoy on 18 July. The division thus no longer had any organized combat units! Small groups tried to link up with German troops. Of the 1,200 men of SS Battle Group Aperats, less than 100 reached the positions of Fusilier Battalion 93 on 20 July 1944.

Not all had been killed or captured. As in the entire division, hundreds of Latvian left their units and tried to reach their homes alone. Those units that could be held together were led into the Karsawa area (approx. 30 km NE of Rositten) and there placed under the commanding officer of the 19th SS Waffen Grenadier Division (Latvian No.2). From there they marched into the Lubahn area and on 23 July handed their remaining heavy weapons over to their sister unit.

On 24 July 1944 Army Group North characterized the two Latvian divisions as *"shattered"* and recommended the disbandment of the 15th SS Waffen Grenadier Division. The surviving members of the division would and could not be deployed at the front again, being used to build positions instead. The Latvian unit had been completely smashed within a few days and had lost the equipment of 15,000 men!

For reasons of prestige, however, Himmler decided not to disband the unit and on 15 August 1944 he issued orders for its reformation in Germany. Every survivor of the division that could be found was ordered to SS Training Camp "Westpreußen" near Zempelburg in the Bütow-Berent area, along with the numerically very strong SS Grenadier Training and Replacement Brigade 15 from Riga.

Following their arrival at the training camp, SS Operational Headquarters ordered the new division commander, the former commanding officer of SS Grenadier Training and Replacement Brigade 15, *SS-Oberführer* von Obwurzer, to restore the unit to operational readiness by 15 November 1944. Von Obwurzer could only be seen as an interim solution, however, as he had demonstrated repeatedly that he lacked the ability to command larger combat units.

After absorbing the approximately 8,000 men of SS Grenadier Training and Replacement Brigade 15, in Kunitz on 20 September 1944 the division was able to report the following strength:

	Officers	NCOs	Enlisted Men	Total
Actual	292	1,522	15,056	16,870
	1.73%	9.02%	89.25%	100%
Authorized	475	2,588	11,619	14,682
	3.24%	17.63%	79.13%	100%

In addition to materiel, the division command was short about 1,500 officers and NCOs to lead its roughly 15,000 men. This shortcoming could not be addressed and seriously reduced the division's operational capability.

It was initially planned that the division should be transferred back to Latvia in November 1944 after a three-month reformation. But as serious problems arose in the procurement of weapons and equipment and the physical condition of the men was very poor[41], it was decided to leave the division at SS Training Camp "Westpreußen". And so the men spent the turn of the year 1944-45 in Germany. Not until *SS-Oberführer* von Obwurzer made his New Year's speech did the men receive a definitive explanation concerning the future of their country:

> "You are fighting for the restoration of an independent Latvia. You are fighting for the liberation of your Latvian homeland, which will become an independent state after the German victory."

---

41 Because of overcrowding of the SS training camp, many men had to be housed in tents. Lack of heating material and inadequate rations soon led to a serious decline in their physical condition.

By that time, however, the statement meant nothing and it is questionable whether the speech was von Obwurzer's own formulation or had been given him by SS Headquarters.

When the Red Army reached Bromberg on 23 January 1945 and no other troops were available, the division had to be placed on alert. It was attached to the newly-formed XVI SS Army Corps (2nd Army), which was organized as follows:

> 15th SS Waffen Grenadier Division (Latvian No. 1)
> SS Volunteer Panzer Grenadier Regiment 48 "General Seyffart"
> "Groß Born" Mixed Artillery Battalion (Motorized)
> 4th Flak Battery 325 (88 mm)
> Latvian Field Replacement Depot[42]
> all troops in the Netze sector

The next day the bulk of the division marched to the front, leaving behind:

> elements of SS Waffen Artillery Regiment 15
> II Battalion, SS Waffen Grenadier Regiment 32
> III Battalion, SS Waffen Grenadier Regiment 33
> II Battalion, SS Waffen Grenadier Regiment 34
> SS Field Replacement Battalion 15

Its orders were to retake Bromberg to the northwest and then occupy position along the Netze River anchored on Bromberg.

Once again anti-tank weapons were in short supply and prevented the Germans from achieving their objectives. *SS-Oberführer* von Obwurzer was killed while driving to the front, and on 25 January 1945 *SS-Oberführer* Ax, chief-of-staff of XVI SS Army Corps, took command of the division. The latter was forced back toward the Vandsburg-Zempelburg area, and both towns were lost on 28 January. Deployed on the 2nd Army's right wing, the XVI SS Army Corps unsuccessfully tried to ensure contact with the left wing of the 11th SS Panzer Army.

On 30 January 1945 the enemy overran the 15th SS Waffen Grenadier Division and forced it in the direction of Neustettin. *SS-Oberführer* Ax issued a halt order, as a result of which the division was briefly encircled in the Flederborn-Ratzebuhr area. It was obvious that Ax was not up to the task of commanding a division. Inflexible halt orders with no contact on either flank inevitably led to encirclement. However, as he had carried out the order to hold the

---

42 The Latvian Field Replacement Depot was directed to send two regiments into the Konitz area and one in the Schneidemühl area as quickly as possible.

area, Ax was awarded the Knight's Cross of the Iron Cross. Then *SS-Obersturmführer* Knöringer remembered:

> "In mid-January 1945 the division, which was resting and refitting, was placed on alert and elements were sent in the direction of the advancing Russians. The situation was so bad that only parts of the division could be sent south by motor transport. The vehicles were fueled in Konitz. In bitter cold in unheated vehicles, we passed through Kamin and Tempelburg and ran into the enemy in the Vandsburg area. At that time the Russians used the following tactic: confident that they would find an empty area, one truck with soldiers and a second with weapons and ammunition would be sent ahead into each of the nearest towns. Consequently our men found themselves facing just a few Russian soldiers and armed civilian auxiliaries. They were overrun and soon our battalions were in Nakel. The Treidel Canal formed the main line of resistance. Our division had no contact with other units on the right or left, and in the days that followed this proved fatal. So what was to be expected had to come!
>
> Several days later the enemy began the dance of survival after a two-hour artillery barrage. After division commander *SS-Oberführer* von Obwurzer was killed, the division fell back to Vandsburg, resisting with all the strength it had. There orders reached us to establish an all-round defense and hold to the last man. It would have been our death sentence had it not been rescinded in time. Obviously some position higher than our division staff was still in existence. Very soon we realized that we were surrounded, and in a "moving pocket" we fought our way on through Wilkenswalde and Flatow to Jastrow.
>
> We had long since ceased to be masters of the situation. The first signs of disintegration began to appear. Enemy units were suddenly in our midst. A few heavy weapons covered us and no one had the time or patience to question the where from and what for. Our regiments were still relatively intact and kept the Russians at a distance. But now we were fighting for our very survival. The enemy forced us back through Flederborn and Wallachsee in the direction of Landeck, where our troops were supposed to be. During those days there were many dispersed units with us, and I would like to make special mention of SS Volunteer Panzer Grenadier Regiment 49. It successfully broke through the Russian lines, the blow that saved us. All of those who survived this chaos owe it a debt of thanks!
>
> Outside Wallachsee, the last town before our main line of resistance, our battalion commander, *SS-Sturmbannführer* Dostmann, summoned all the men with all the remaining weapons. Only the drivers remained in their vehicles. He assembled about 50 men at the edge of the forest. We observed the ground before us shrouded in deepest darkness and knew: that's where the Russian anti-tank guns are. We could just make

Romans Riekstins – a namesake of the Knight's Cross wearer Alfreds Riekstins – joined SS Waffen Artillery Regiment 15 (Latvian No.1) on 5 August 1944. He was promoted to Waffen-Sturmmann on 11 February 1945.

On 24 January 1945 the bulk of the 15th SS Waffen Grenadier Division marched to the front near Nakel on the Netze River. While on the move they were subjected to persistent Soviet air attacks. Romans Riekstins succeeded in bringing down an enemy aircraft with small arms fire and the same day was awarded the Special Badge for the Shooting Down of Aircraft with Small Arms. He was also given an early promotion to Waffen-Sturmmann.

out the outlines of several buildings. At dawn *SS-Sturmbannführer* Dostmann and a few men crept along the edge of the forest and reached the road out of the village on the other side. I then assembled 10 to 15 men around me and headed the same way, however I was surprised by the dawn. We took cover behind the trees and observed a sawmill. All was quiet. Slowly the outlines of the buildings appeared before us. There was no movement.

Of the other units of the division, there was nothing to be seen or heard anywhere. Suddenly there was a deafening outburst of battle noise. From the opposing hills to the west the enemy was firing everything he had at the meadow in front of us. With the ten to fifteen brave Latvians who had been forced into battle with almost no infantry training, we captured the buildings east of the through road. The enemy held the houses opposite. We were forced to fall back with heavy casualties. Among the dead was *SS-Sturmbannführer* Dostmann. Meanwhile our vehicle column was backed up on the road. An 88-mm anti-aircraft gun went into position and held the Russians at bay.

From there the road to Landeck was completely treeless for about two kilometers and was entirely under enemy fire. Our 1st General Staff Officer therefore authorized only single vehicles to take the road and each tried to dash to the safety of the forest.

I rode for some distance on the fender of a staff vehicle. Then it was hit by anti-tank fire and halted on the open road. In addition to my personal things I lost all of the battalion's personnel papers (service records). My driver and I escaped with a few cuts and bruises and joined the column, which was halted in the forest. A 75-mm anti-tank gun of SS Volunteer Panzer Grenadier Regiment 48 was positioned at a slight bend in the road, and it blasted a way clear. Despite many casualties, most reached the saving bridge to Landeck and the main line of resistance on the other side."

On 3 February 1945 the unit reached Landeck and one week later XVIII Mountain Corps took command from headquarters, XVI SS Army Corps, which was disbanded. The badly battered 15th SS Waffen Grenadier Division was now sent to Group Ax and consisted of:

 Division Headquarters
 Battle Group "Scheibe"
  remnants of Grenadier Regiment 59
  remnants of SS Volunteer Panzer Grenadier Regiment 48
  2 alert battalions
 Battle Group "Janums"
  remnants of the 15th SS Waffen Grenadier Division (Latvian No.1)
  2 alert battalions

Gruppe "Ax" had no heavy weapons and was used purely in the infantry role. It faced Soviet air power, artillery and tanks with carbines, machine-guns and Panzerfausts. Nevertheless, on 15 February 1945 Gruppe "Ax" launched a limited counterattack towards the east from the area east of Neustettin and managed to stabilize the front, at least temporarily. *SS-Oberführer* Burk from the officer reserve subsequently took command of the mixed group and three days later led it into the Prützenwalde area. There positions were supposed to be built between Landeck and Küddow. On 24 February the Red Army broke through the positions of the 32nd Infantry Division on the left wing, and the battle group was forced to abandon its positions. At the same time, SS Grenadier Training and Replacement Battalion 15, which was still at the training camp in Berent, was attached to Group von Rappard (C.O. 7th Infantry Division). Like the remaining elements of the 15th SS Waffen Grenadier Division in Konitz, it was forced into the Danzig area.

On 26 February 1945 fierce fighting also developed near Hammerstein. The division was attached to Corps Group "Tettau", which formed the left wing of the 3rd Panzer Army in positions extending to the Baltic. Marching through Gramenz into the Belgard area, the corps group was almost encircled. While it attempted to regain contact with the German lines, conditions again became chaotic. With no firm control over his units, *Generalleutnant* von Tettau, the commanding general of the corps group, saw no other possibility than to order the destruction of all remaining weapons and vehicles and his men to make their way toward the west in small groups. After briefly manning improvised defense positions between Lake Wilm, Lake Dolgen and Steppen, on 11 March 1945 the remnants of the 15th SS Waffen Grenadier Division reached the bridgehead at Dievenow. Operational elements were briefly attached to Corps Group "Munzel" for use in the bridgehead position. On 19 March the men left the combat zone and followed the other division elements to Mecklenburg. At that time the 15th SS Waffen Grenadier Division was organized into remnant units as follows:

    SS Waffen Grenadier Regiment 32 (2 battalions)
    SS Waffen Grenadier Regiment 33 (2 battalions)
    SS Waffen Grenadier Regiment 34 (2 battalions)
    SS Fusilier Battalion (2 companies)
    SS Artillery Battalion (no weapons, personnel only)
    SS Anti-tank Battalion (no weapons, personnel only)

Ordered into the Fürstenberg-Feldberg-Lychen area, the Latvians were placed under *Generalleutnant* Denecke, commander of the rear army area (*Korück*), 3rd Panzer Army. While the bulk of the unit was used to construct positions in the rear near Neustrelitz, volunteers from the grenadier regiments were used to form a battalion-strength battle group. Reinforced by a company from SS Fusilier Battalion 15, the battle group was dispatched to the XI SS Panzer Corps in Herzfelde (north of Erkner). Contrary to German orders, the commander of the battle group. *Waffen-Standartenführer* Janums, led his men (40 officers, 126 NCOs and 658 enlisted men) northwest past Berlin. Near Gutergluck on the Elbe they surrendered to American forces.

Only the company from Fusilier Battalion 15 marched to Berlin, where it took part in the final battles, lastly at the State Ministry of Aviation. The remaining units of the 15th SS Waffen Grenadier Division were ordered to build positions on Lake Malchin and on 2 May moved to the Schweriner Forest. There they surrendered to forces of the western allies.

On 23 January 1945 three grenadier battalions and an artillery battalion had stayed behind at the SS Training Camp "Westpreußen". At the end of February they were attached to the 227th Infantry Division, which, as part of XXXXVI Panzer Corps (2nd Army), was withdrawing toward the area. Without being drawn into combat, the approximately 3,000 Latvians marched northeast toward Karthaus. From there, moving over congested roads, they reached the Sargosch-Groß Katz area and were put to work building positions. The Red Army breached the main line of resistance on 12 March. With the enemy advance to the Baltic, VII Panzer Corps assumed command in the area, which had been declared "Fortress Gotenhafen". On 20 March 1945 the Latvians were divided among German battle groups and drawn into the defense. The bulk of the men were captured by the Soviets. Only about 500 were evacuated by sea to Swinemünde and followed the remnant division into the Neustrelitz area.

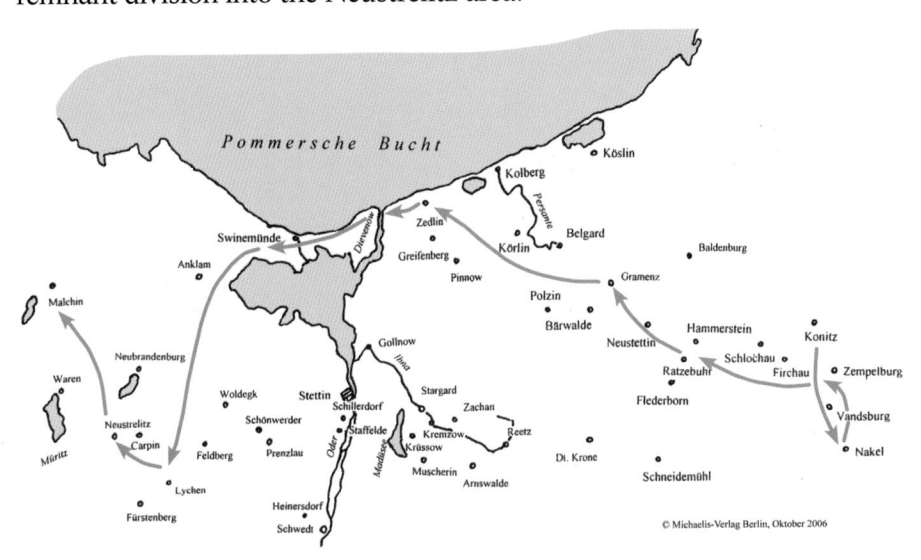

The 15th SS Waffen Grenadier Division's withdrawal through Pomerania in February-March 1945.

Special pass for Waffen-Sturmmann Janis Bezags and Waffen-Grenadier Alfons Podratnicks to report to the 15th SS Waffen Grenadier Division (Latvian No.1)'s collection point in Neubrandenburg. Note the addendum, according to which Waffen-Sturmmann Podratnicks "left transport" – in other words deserted.

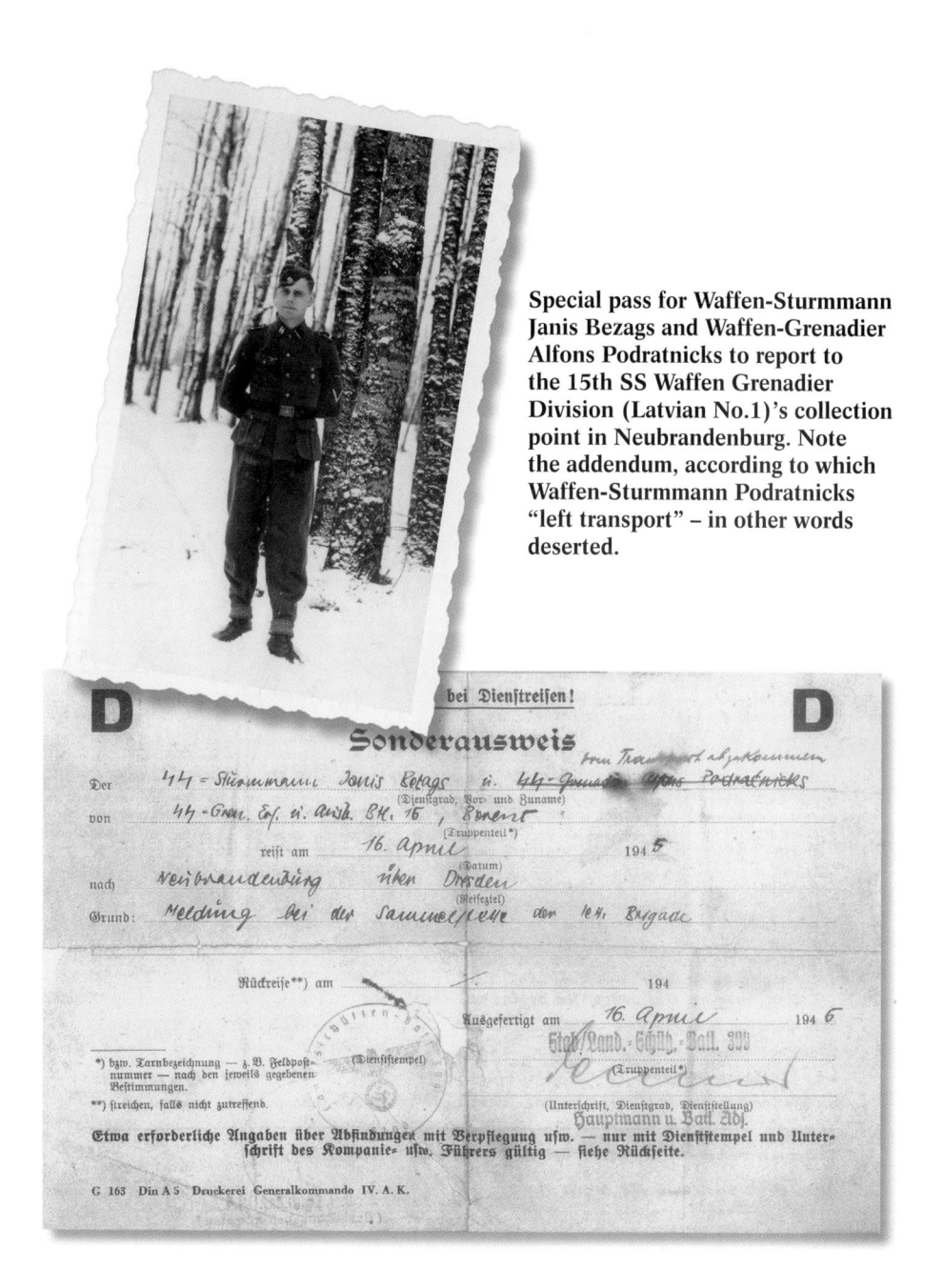

The division was formed at a time when the beginning of the end was at hand. Production bottlenecks in the armament industry plus a shortage of capable commanders denied success to the unit, which consisted of men who, as in 1918, saw Germany as a lesser evil than Russia. The basic motivation, as after the First World War, was the desire for sovereignty. Thus, even though they had served in the Waffen-SS, after a victory over Russia the men would surely have turned against Germany if necessary, as in 1919.

As members of a so-called foreign unit of the *Waffen-SS*, the division's personnel were supposed to receive a special collar patch. Instead of Sigrunen, it bore a stylized sun and three stars for Courland, Livonia and Latgalia (note the portrait photo in the paybook above). In fact, however, most men wore the collar patch with the Sigrunen.

Waffen-Sturmmann Lecis joined SS Volunteer Regiment 3 of the Latvian SS Volunteer Division on 27 July 1943 and from 11 September 1944 was attached to the 3rd (Convalescent) Company of SS Grenadier Training and Replacement Battalion 15.

On 13 September 1943, *SS-Obergruppenführer* and General der *Polizei* Jeckeln, the Senior SS and Police Commander for Ostland, advised that Himmler had authorized the Latvian SS volunteers to wear the Latvian national emblem with the script "Latvia". The badge was always worn on the right upper sleeve.

Initially all members of the Latvian SS Volunteer Legion wore a national shield on the right upper sleeve. Numerous variations of the shield were produced.

A standardized national shield was introduced in June 1944. It was supposed to be worn on the left upper sleeve with the eagle sewed on about 5 cm higher.

Members of the 15th SS Waffen Grenadier Division after the end of the war.

The 2nd Latvian SS Volunteer Brigade

Die 2. Lettishe SS-Freiwilligen-Brigade

Many Latvian volunteers showed no desire to extend their formal obligations to serve in the *Schutzmannschafts* battalions. This, together with a desire for a Latvian military unit, fostered the idea of creating an alternative to the *Schutzmannschafts* battalions within the Waffen-SS.

When Hitler ordered the formation of a Latvian SS Volunteer Legion in February 1943, *Schutzmannschafts* Battalions 19 and 21, both of which were serving within the 2nd SS Motorized Infantry Brigade in front of eningrad, became the I and II Battalions of the Latvian Legion.

For propaganda reasons, the Germans wished to give the Latvians the illusion of serving in a national formation, consequently the unit was initially called the Latvian Legion, with no reference to the Waffen-SS. Rank designations did change, however, to those of the Waffen-SS, although the "SS" was replaced by "Legionäre" (e.g. *Legions-Sturmmann* or *Legions-Untersturmführer*).

On 29 March 1943 *Schutzmannschafts* Battalion 16 became the III Battalion of the Latvian Legion and was sent to Pulkovo in the siege line around Leningrad, where the other two battalions were already stationed. With numerous Waffen-SS units being formed, it was decided to turn the multinational[43] 2nd SS Motorized Infantry Brigade into a homogenous Latvian formation. In April 1943 *Schutzmannschafts* Battalions 18, 24 and 26 were sent to the Krasnoye Selo area to form the second grenadier regiment. In the weeks that followed, remnants and elements of the Latvian *Schutzmannschafts* Battalions 27, 28, 267, 268, 269, 272, 280, 281 and 311 were used to bring the regiments up to authorized strength and form the brigade's supporting units and supply elements.

At the end of April 1943 the brigade was ordered to the XXXVIII Army Corps in the Krechno area (NW of Novgorod). This was followed on 18 May 1943 by the order to renamed the 2nd SS Motorized Infantry Brigade the Latvian SS Volunteer Brigade. Commanded by *SS-Brigadeführer* von Scholz, the unit was organized into:

> Brigade Headquarters
> 4th and 5th SS Volunteer Regiments (each I – III Battalions)
> SS Artillery Battalion
> SS Flak Battalion
> SS Anti-Tank Battalion (H.Q. and 1 company)
> SS Pioneer Company
> SS Signals Company

---

43 Dutch and Flemish soldiers served alongside Latvians in the brigade.

SS Medical Company
SS Supply Company
SS Field Replacement Company

There was no serious fighting in the brigade's sector until the summer of 1943. At the beginning of September 1943 the Red Army took the offensive, and within a week the brigade suffered casualties of 145 killed and 650 wounded. On 4 September 1943 *SS-Brigadeführer* Schuldt relieved the previous commander *SS-Brigadeführer* von Scholz, who had been given command of the SS Volunteer Panzer Grenadier Division *"Nordland"*.

On 22 October 1943, in the course of the consecutive numbering of Waffen-SS units, the brigade received the number 2 and its official designation became 2nd Latvian SS Volunteer Brigade. The two regiments were simultaneously renamed SS Volunteer Grenadier Regiment 39 (Latvian No.1) and 40 (Latvian No.2). They were given the numbers 1 and 2 because they were the first two Latvian regiments to see action. Still deployed northwest of Lake Ilmen, on 31 December 1943 the brigade submitted the following strength report:

Officers	NCOs	Enlisted Men	Total
239	1,133	6,661	8,033
3.0%	14.1%	82.9%	100%

The units were thus over authorized strengths, and the brigade had a foundation which could be quickly expanded into a division.

THE 19TH SS WAFFEN GRENADIER DIVISION (LATVIAN NO.2)

When it was realized that, with general mobilization in Latvia imminent, this expansion could be achieved, at least quantitatively, in a short time, on 7 January 1944 Himmler ordered the brigade reorganized as the **19th Latvian SS Volunteer Division.** Its proposed organization was:

Division Headquarters
SS Volunteer Regiment 42[44] (Latvian No. 1) with I – III Battalions
SS Volunteer Regiment 43 (Latvian No. 2) with I – III Battalions
SS Volunteer Regiment 44 (Latvian No. 6) with I – III Battalions
SS Volunteer Artillery Regiment 19 (I – IV Battalions)
SS Anti-Tank Battalion 19 (just 1 company due to equipment shortages)
SS Signals Battalion 19
SS Field Replacement Battalion 19

---

[44] The numbering changed as a result of the formation of new SS divisions.

SS Flak Battalion 19
SS Fusilier Battalion 19
SS Economic Battalion 19
SS Medical Battalion 19

As the unit could not be pulled out of action for reorganization, however, initially it retained the composition of the 2nd Latvian SS Volunteer Brigade.

The Soviets launched their winter offensive on 14 January 1944. The Red Army penetrated deep into the main line of resistance of the 1st Field Division (L) of the same XXXVIII Army Corps. Under the command of *Legions-Standartenführer* Veiss, I Battalion, SS Volunteer Grenadier Regiment 39 and III Battalion, SS Volunteer Grenadier Regiment 40 saved encircled *Wehrmacht* elements from destruction. In the fierce defensive fighting that followed, Battle Group "Veiss" and II and III Battalions of SS Volunteer Grenadier Regiment 39 were forced to pull back, while I and II Battalions of SS Volunteer Grenadier Regiment 40 initially remained in their positions. On 21 January these two battalions also gave up the main line of resistance and withdrew through Finyev Lug and Pristani to Orodesch, covering the rest of the brigade's retreat.

On 2 February 1944 the units of the 2nd Latvian SS Volunteer Brigade occupied positions on either side of Orodesch and covered the retreat by German units in the direction of Luga. Falling back under tremendous pressure from the Red Army, on 12 February the Latvian volunteers reached Luga. The retreat continued, with the brigade falling back toward Stinya (NW of Dno) until 22 February. The brigade continued to cover the retreat until the "Panther Position" along the Velikaya River near Ostrov was reached and occupied on 26 February. In the past six weeks, not only had the Latvian volunteers maintained their cohesion and retained the bulk of their equipment, but they had also inflicted heavy losses on the Soviet troops. On 29 February 1944 the *Wehrmacht* communiqué declared:

> "In the fierce defensive fighting in the northern sector of the Eastern Front, the 2nd Latvian SS Volunteer Brigade under the command of Oak Leaves wearer *SS-Oberführer* Schuldt and its Latvian infantry commander, the Knight's Cross wearer *SS-Standartenführer* Veiss, particularly distinguished themselves."

The then *SS-Unterscharführer* Gerhard Nitzschke remembered:

> "After attending the Waffen-SS administration school, in August 1942 I was assigned to the office of the SS and Police Commander "Caucasus". In May 1943 I was transferred to the Latvian SS Volunteer Brigade, then being formed, as accounting officer. The members of the brigade, which later became the 19th SS Waffen Grenadier Division, were generally

good and in some cases fanatical fighters. As a Latvian supply NCO told me, many of the men had lost family members as a result of the events of 1940. When the Russian campaign began, the supply NCO was in Moscow attending a teacher conference and was immediately drafted. He was captured by the Germans in one of the first battles of encirclement, and after his release he volunteered to serve in one of the auxiliary police battalions, which was then attached to the 2nd SS Motorized Infantry Brigade. One night our later commander, Captain Schuldt as we call him, ordered that the administrative officers should bring the coffee and rations to the positions. That earned him a great deal of respect among the grenadiers. When the retreat began in 1944, the headquarters staff of our SS Volunteer Regiment 40 was evacuated in panye wagons over the log roads. There were no vehicles for some groups, such as the IV a [supply officer]. We therefore had to take the "Volkhov narrow gauge railroad" to Glukhaya – Karesty and from there further to the rear. We waited at the station and no train came. Suddenly a report went through the ranks that the Russians had broken through, no more trains were coming. Panic-stricken, we took our most important personal things and fled towards the rear. In the next village several comrades and I organized a sleigh with horses and got out of there as quickly as we could. Unfortunately we had no idea where the front was and we definitely didn't want to fall into the hands of the Russians. The liquor casks in the supply depot were opened, in the hope that the Russians would stop to drink their fill and in this way delay their advance. As a result of our hasty departure we lost contact with the other units and it wasn't until Ostrov that we again found the regiment."

In the "Panther Position" it was combined with the 15th Latvian SS Volunteer Division and the 12th Field Division (L) under the VI SS Volunteer Army Corps (Latvian). In mid-March 1944[45] the Red Army attacked on the plateau between Ostrov and Opochka. *SS-Brigadeführer* Schuldt was killed in the fighting on 15 March, and two days later the *Wehrmacht* communiqué declared:

> "On the remaining Eastern Front the Soviets attacked in the area west of Nevel, near Ostrov and on the Narva front. Latvian SS volunteer units played a prominent part in fighting off these attacks."

The fighting near Petschane Hill (Hill 93.4), which represented the boundary between the two Latvian SS units, was particularly fierce. The *Wehrmacht* communiqué of 27 March 1944 reported:

---

45 In 1999 the Latvian parliament declared 16 March the "Day of the Soldiers" in memory of the veterans who fought against the USSR in the Second World War.

> "In the area south of Ostrov, Latvian SS volunteer units, together with German troops, repulsed assaults by several enemy divisions. A local penetration was sealed off."

Two days later the Latvians were again mentioned in the *Wehrmacht* communiqué:

> "In heavy fighting, heavy enemy attacks were repulsed by German troops and Latvian SS volunteer units southeast of Ostrov and on the Narva front."

The reports were very euphemistic, for despite heavy losses the Red Army was able to reach its operational objective, the Velikaya River south of Pskov, and establish a bridgehead there. On 10 April the Soviets temporarily halted their offensive. The 2nd Latvian SS Volunteer Division was officially still in the formation stage, and as it had been badly battered in the fighting, Army Group North ordered its accelerated restoration and completion of the expansion into a division in the area southwest of Novorzhev (approx. 75 km SE of Ostrov).

In the course of the formation of the 19th Latvian SS Volunteer Division the third regiment was formed using a battalion from each of the first two grenadier regiments. The third battalions were all new formations, which were supposed to be sent to the division from Latvia. Other units arrived in the formation area during the almost three months of rest and restoration, including a II (Light) Artillery Battalion. Another light battalion and a heavy artillery battalion were still being formed in Vainode.

While the unit forged ahead with training and built positions in the area of the front, in June 1944 it was renamed the **19th SS Waffen Grenadier Division (Latvian No.2)** and the regiments retitled SS Waffen Grenadier/Artillery Regiments. The division's reported strength was:

	Officers	NCOs	Enlisted Men	Total
Actual	329	1,421	8,842	10,592
	3.1%	13.4%	83.5%	100%
Authorized	473	2,587	11,615	14,675
	3.2%	17.6%	79.2%	100%

It was thus more than 4,000 men below authorized strength. As several units were still being raised in Latvia, however, it was assured that the division would achieve its authorized strength at a later date. *SS-Brigadeführer* Streckenbach was named division commander and this officer would lead the division for the rest of the war.

Exactly three years after the German attack on the Soviet Union, on 22 June 1944 the Russians launched their summer offensive. On 10 July 1944, in the second phase of their offensive, the Soviets also attacked in the area of the VI SS Waffen Army Corps (Latvian). Deployed on the left wing of the 16th Army, it had had barely tens weeks of rest and was supposed to be an effective defensive fighting force. The 19th SS Waffen Grenadier Division did in fact hold its lines against the powerful enemy attacks, however the neighboring 15th SS Waffen Grenadier Division quickly collapsed.

The next day *SS-Gruppenführer* Treuenfeld, commanding general of the VI SS Waffen Army Corps (Latvian), ordered a retreat to the Odenwald Position, and contact was lost with the 18th Army to the north, resulting in the so-called "Latvian gap". Instead of offering resistance to the Soviets, the front began to move. Powerful enemy armored formations immediately drove into the retreat, creating chaos among the Latvian-German troops. It was impossible to lead the units in an organized defense. Instead, on 13 July 1944 the Latvian war volunteers crossed the Velikaya near Opochka. As some swam the Velikaya in their headlong flight, large quantities of heavy equipment were left on the east bank of the river, where they fell into enemy hands.

On 16 July 1944 what was left of the 19th SS Waffen Grenadier Division reached its Latvian homeland and briefly manned defense positions in the Karsava-Merdzene (approx. 20 km N of Ludsen) area. There the remnants of its sister unit were attached to the division. Three days later the Latvian units were reorganized into Division Group "Streckenbach". From the three regiment's total of nine grenadier battalions, just three battalion-strength regimental groups could be formed, mainly because of the desertion of hundreds of Latvians. On 24 July 1944 Army Group North characterized the 19th SS Waffen Grenadier Division as *"shattered"*. However, as it still had its division commander (sic!), it assumed command of operational elements of the 15th SS Waffen Grenadier Division (in particular two Artillery battalions with personnel). Marching to the west north of Rositten, Group "Streckenbach" occupied positions on either side of Lake Lubahne (approx. 170 km E of Riga).

On 1 August 1944, SS Field Replacement Battalion 19 had to be sent to the front to strengthen the units there. It was later renamed SS Fusilier Battalion 19. After powerful attacks by the Red Army, on 5 August 1944 Group "Streckenbach" withdrew across the Aiviekste in the direction of Modohn-Vesvaine (German Seswegen, approx. 18 km N of Modohn). In constant danger of being overtaken and destroyed by Soviet troops, the group was able to occupy temporary defense positions in this area. The following supplemental report to the *Wehrmacht* communiqué was issued on 9 August 1944:

Final inspection and first action at the front for Latvian SS volunteers. Below: camouflaging a 75mm Pak 40 anti-tank gun.

"In the northern sector of the Eastern Front, the North-German 83rd Infantry Division under Oberst Gölz with attached elements of the East Prussian 61st Infantry Division and the 19th Latvian SS Division under the command of *SS-Brigadeführer* and *Generalmajor der Waffen-SS* Streckenbach have distinguished themselves in attack and defense."

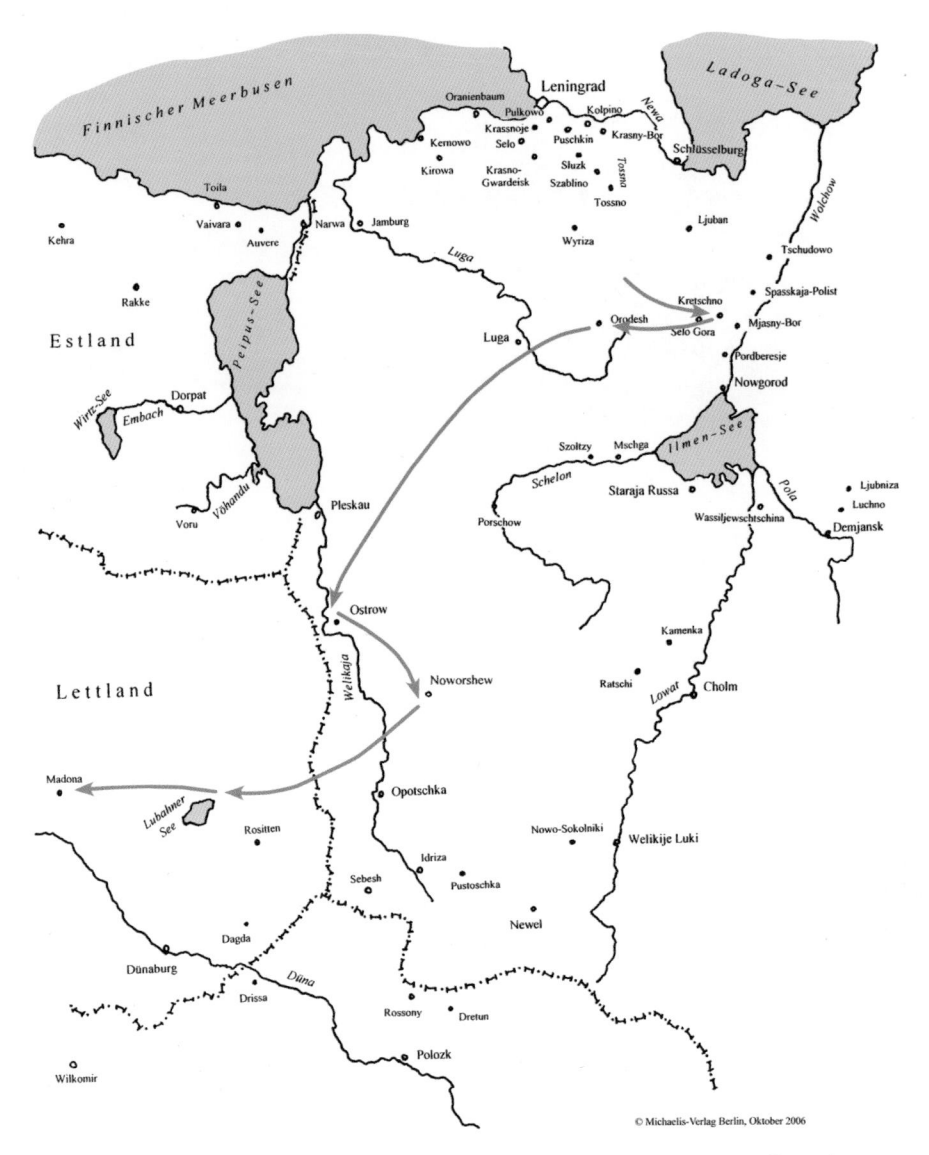

There was fierce fighting along the Modohn-Cervaine line until 21 August. After several days of quiet the enemy resumed his attacks, took Modohn and forced Group "Streckenbach" to fall back to the northwest through Schwanenburg (Latvian Gulbene) behind the Tirza. Nevertheless, on 16 September 1944 the *Wehrmacht* communiqué reported:

> "In the areas of Bauske, Modohn and Walk the Soviets, supported by tanks and close-support aviation, resumed their heavy attacks. Side by side with Latvian volunteer units and in outstanding cooperation with the Luftwaffe, our divisions frustrated every attempt by the enemy to break through."

Funeral services and burial of fallen members of the Latvian SS Volunteer Legion in Latvia.

After moving into the Segewold Position (approx. 50 km NE of Riga), large numbers of replacements were integrated into the units. The regimental groups, for example, were brought almost to regiment strength. The division was able to submit the following strength report on 20 September 1944:[46]

	Officers	NCOs	Enlisted Men	Total
Actual	414	1,974	10,119	12,507
	3.3%	15.8%	80.9%	100%
Authorized	473	2,587	11,615	14,675
	3.2%	17.6%	79.2%	100%

The 19th SS Waffen Grenadier Division (Latvian No.2) was at least numerically strong. In fact, most of the men had been sent to the front from a replacement depot and had no war experience. The unit's fighting strength thus had to be regarded as rather low.

The fighting for the Segewold Position continued at the end of September 1944. The Latvians achieved numerous defensive successes. This was all the more amazing as the bulk of the units consisted of inexperienced men. The *Wehrmacht* released the following supplement to its daily report on 30 September 1944:

> "In the defensive struggle in Latvia, the 19th SS Waffen Grenadier Division (Latvian No.2) under the command of *SS-Brigadeführer* and *Generalmajor der Waffen-SS* Streckenbach has performed magnificently in the defense of its native soil."

After Hitler authorized the withdrawal of German units from Livonia and Latgalia to the Courland, on 7 October 1944 the 19th SS Waffen Grenadier Division received orders to abandon its lines in the Segewold Position. It briefly left the VI SS Waffen Army Corps (Latvian) and moved into the Doblin area (approx 35 km W of Mitau) to the 16th Army's threatened right wing. It was followed there by the newly-formed SS Waffen Grenadier Regiment 106 (Latvian No.7). Designated a corps unit, it was initially attached to the division. As part of Corps Group "Kleffel", beginning 15 October 1944 the division took part in heavy fighting against the Red Army (First Battle of Courland). The Soviets committed huge quantities of materiel in an attempt to force

---

46 The unit had received a large number of replacements in a short time. In addition to recruits drafted in the spring of 1944, a Latvian battle group under the command of *SS-Hauptsturmführer* Fritz Ulrich, a member of the SD, was also integrated. Of the 15th SS Waffen Grenadier Division (Latvian No.1), two artillery battalions and SS Pioneer Battalion 15 were attached to the 19th Division.

a quick decision in Courland. The 19th SS Waffen Grenadier Division found itself in the thick of the fighting. Losses were heavy, and the lines had to be withdrawn with front facing east. Among the measures taken to strengthen the units, *Schutzmannschafts* Front Battalion 271 was integrated into SS Waffen Grenadier Regiment 43.

The enemy subsequently shifted his operational objective and the area held by the 19th SS Waffen Grenadier Division remained relatively quiet during the 2nd Battle of Courland. After Hitler had abandoned large parts of Latvia, fear spread among the population and the volunteers that Germany would quickly withdraw from Courland. Many soldiers therefore left their units and returned to their families.

On 23 December 1944, during the Third Battle of Courland, the VI SS Waffen Army Corps came under heavy attack. By then the corps had the following units under its command:

>   93rd Infantry Division
>   19th SS Waffen Grenadier Division
>   Group "Barth" [remnants of the 21st Field Division (L)] with attached SS Waffen Grenadier Regiment 106 (Latvian No. 7)

After serious penetrations against Group "Barth", under the weight of the enemy offensive the main line of resistance had to be withdrawn about four kilometers to the west to a point just outside Lestene (approx. 30 km N of Doblen). When the Soviet offensive lost impetus, on 5 and 6 January 1945 the VI SS Waffen Army Corps (Latvian) counterattacked and gained ground. After the 93rd Infantry Division

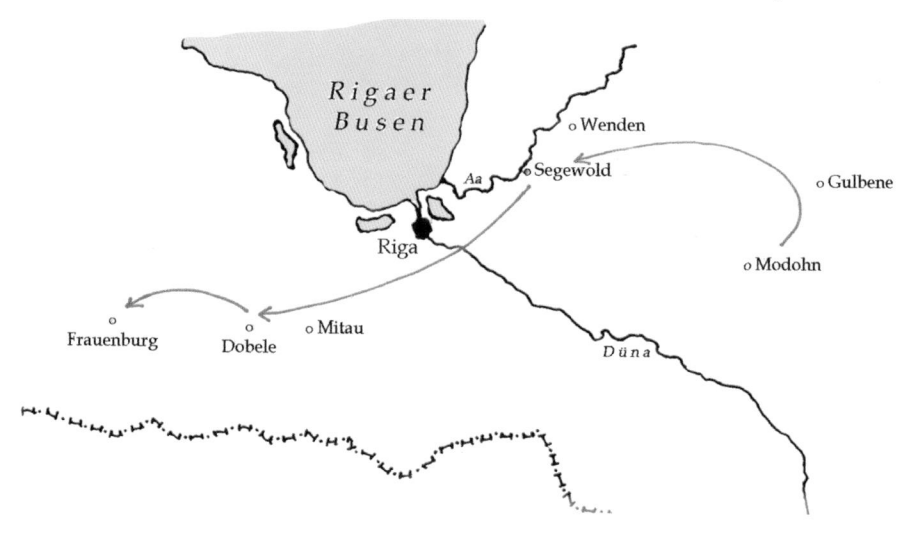

Area of operations of the 19th SS Waffen Grenadier Division (Latvian No.2) from October 1944 to May 1945.

Members of the Latvian SS Volunteer Legion.

was moved to Germany in January 1945, the 19th SS Waffen Grenadier Division took over positions of its neighbor on the right. The main line of resistance, which was about 15 km long, ran from Dzukste (German Siuxt) to Jaunpils (German Neuenburg).

In order to increase the motivation of the Latvian volunteers and provide a visual recognition of the fighting spirit they had demonstrated, on 15 January 194 SS Waffen Grenadier Regiment 42

80

(Latvian No. 1[47]) was given the name "Voldermars Veiss", after the fallen first Latvian winner of the Knight's Cross. SS Waffen Grenadier Regiment 43 (Latvian No.2) was honored with the name of the fallen commander of the 2nd Latvian SS Volunteer Brigade "Hinrich Schuldt". There was not time, however, to create corresponding cuff titles.

When the Red Army failed to achieve a decisive success in this sector of the front, for the Fourth Battle of Courland (23 January to 3 February 1945) it shifted its main effort to the area around Preekuln. The Fifth Battle of Courland began in the same area a few days later (12 February to 10 March 1945). As it went on the focus shifted to the east and led to fierce attacks against the 19th SS Waffen Grenadier Division. The division was forced to withdraw its left wing toward the Irlava area (approx. 15 km NW of Lestene). As well, SS Fusilier Battalion 19 was attached to SS Waffen Grenadier Regiment 106 of Group "Barth" after the latter's fighting strength was reduced almost to zero.

There was further fighting one week later, when, during the course of the Sixth Battle of Courland (17 March to 4 April 1945), the Red Army launched an attack toward Saldus (German Frauenburg). When the Soviets succeeded in breaking through the German position near Blidene (approx. 15 km NE of Saldus), elements of SS Waffen Grenadier Regiment 42 were moved into the hotly contested area approximately 20 km to the west. Units of SS Waffen Grenadier Regiment 42 followed into the Kaulaci area (approx. 3 km NW of Blidene) and of the SS Waffen Grenadier Regiment into the Saldus area. These, together with units of the 24th and 218th Infantry Divisions, were able to at least seal off the enemy penetrations. When the Red Army subsequently took the offensive in the Jaunpils area, the division was forced to create alert units from rear-echelon services to bolster its weakened left wing. Despite heavy fighting, it was largely able to hold its positions. When this offensive petered out, it was the end of the fighting in Courland.

On 7 May 1945 the 19th SS Waffen Grenadier Division had an infantry strength of about 3,500 men. That was roughly equal to 60% of its authorized strength of 6,000 men in the three grenadier regiments. If one assumes that the infantry force was raised for the most part by secondments from the supply units, then on the day of the surrender the division had something over 8,000 men. In heavy weapons the unit still had:

---

47 The chronological numbering of the Latvian grenadier regiments was repeatedly changed, and numerically some of the regiments of the 15th SS Division came before those of the 19th Division, though the first two regiments of the Latvian SS Volunteer Legion to see action were designated "Latvian No.1 and 2". In the late summer of 1944 the first two regiments of the 19th SS Waffen Grenadier Division again received the designations "Latvian No.1 and 2".

- 6 75mm anti-tank guns
- 9 light artillery batteries
- 3 heavy artillery batteries

Only part of the division's personnel laid down their weapons on 8 May 1945. The bulk tried to escape imprisonment, went into the forests, fought as partisans against the Red Army or tried to assume new identities. Those captured by the Soviets were deported to Siberia or Karelia until the 1950s. The last so-called "Forest Brothers", who were often supported by the Latvian population and operated in the forests against the reestablished communist regime, stopped fighting in the 1950s. Former *SS-Untersturmführer* Grawe remembered:

> "Born on 31 October 1923, on 1 February 1941 I joined the SS Death's Head Replacement Battalion I. In 1943 I was transferred to the SS Court Head Office and from there in April 1943 to the field court of the 19th Latvian SS Volunteer Division as head of the administrative office. I travelled over muddy roads and when I reached the division it was involved in heavy defensive fighting in the Ostrov area. There I met Veiss and Schuldt. The latter was described to me as a father to the troops, and the impression he made was exactly that. Sadly both men were killed a few weeks later.
>
> Our headquarters section was billeted in one of the many typical villages. I believe it was called Medvedevo. The residents displayed no open hostility. Although we were often totally cut off because of the impassibility of the roads, there were no problems with partisans. In one village I even acted as village judge on one occasion. The village elder wanted me to arbitrate disputes between married couples and neighbors. Fortunately I was able to restore peace.
>
> The large-scale withdrawals and defensive battles began in July-August 1944 and subsequently ended in Courland. We were constantly on the move until October 1944. In daylight foot marches, often completely on our own, our headquarters section made its way back across the Dvina. The regiments of the division had it particularly tough, because they had to fight off the pursuing Russians.
>
> The defensive battle in Courland began in early October 1944. Our section took up quarters in Irlava. We built hedgehog positions for all-round defense and formed alert platoons, which were often employed to seal off penetrations.
>
> At our last meeting with division commander Streckenbach, he informed us that he had given the order to begin surrender negotiations, but that it was being ignored by some Latvian commanders. The units would disband and go their own way. We were also left to make our own decisions.

> In the end there was no other way except the one into captivity. For me this meant more than five years behind barbed wire. In December 1949 a war tribunal in Zhitomir sentenced me to 25 years in a labor camp for being a member of the 19th SS Waffen Grenadier Division. Nevertheless, in 1950 I was unexpectedly released."

Formed from former auxiliary policemen of the *Ordnungspolizei*, the 2nd Latvian SS Volunteer Brigade and later the 19th SS Waffen Grenadier Division (Latvian No.2) formed a capable cadre which was bolstered by recruits. Constantly employed in a defensive role, it was adequately equipped for a grenadier division. More Knight's Crosses of the Iron Cross were awarded to members of the 2nd Latvian SS Volunteer Brigade and the 19th SS Waffen Grenadier Division (Latvian No.2) than to any other foreign unit. Even if some of the decorations were awarded for propaganda reasons, they showed the motivation with which the Latvians fought against the Red Army. Former Waffen-Obersturm*führer* Teodors Kalnajs recalls his military career, from serving in a *Schutzmannschafts* battalion to the 19th SS Waffen Grenadier Division (Latvian No.2):

> "Our *Schutzmannschafts* Battalion 24 occupied position right at the front before Leningrad. An Estonian said to me: this isn't the famous "iron ring", it's a "rubber ring"… We dug in and built wooden bunkers, half buried in the ground and fortified from without by sand. Fierce storms set in in November 1942. The water in the nearby bay came over the banks and flooded the flat area. There was also light snow, and our bunkers ended up full of water. We ended up sitting on the tables—the water rose to the edge of the table. The trenches filled with water and even the rats ran away… In March-April 1943 two regiments were formed from the six battalions on the Leningrad front and moved to the Volkhov. There it was all swamps and moors—digging in was impossible. The bodies of fallen soldiers lay everywhere; in the spring they thawed out and decomposed, creating an unbearable stench. The front remained quiet until September 1943. Then the Russian offensive broke loose and we lost 700 killed and wounded in a few days! We were pulled out of our position and received replacements. I was wounded and brought to Riga. I was thus out of the quagmire and was assigned to the 3rd Grenadier Regiment for the 19th Latvian SS Volunteer Division. The new recruits received almost no training and the regiment, whose 8th Company I commanded, was ordered to the front on 4 March 1944. There were fierce battles on 16 March. As these were the only ones in which the 15th and 19th SS Volunteer Divisions fought the Red Army together, this day was later celebrated as the "Day of the Legion". My company and I covered the regiment's retreat toward the Segewold Position, for which I was decorated…

From there we then withdrew into the Doblen area and there built good positions. Our men went to church and used the sauna. A big offensive started on 23 December 1944. On the first day our area was still quiet, but then the front of the 21st Luftwaffe Field Division cracked and we became involved in heavy fighting.

Then I became aide-de-camp in the regimental headquarters. One time a grenadier brought in a Russian prisoner, perhaps a deserter. It turned out that he was Latvian. When we asked him if he wanted to fight on our side he said no, he didn't want to shoot at all any more. One day the telephone rang and our division commander Streckenbach told me that the war was over. I immediately woke my regimental commander Praulins and told him that Germany had surrendered! I saw no white flags among us, we pulled back. The Red Army troops climbed out of their trenches and advanced. We took from the supply dump what we could carry, intending to go into the forests. We thought that the Americans or English would come to protect Latvia from being occupied again. We were wrong! While many wanted to fight the Red Army as partisans—what alternative did they have?—I met a friend who could issue me "good" documents. They didn't help for long, however. I was arrested by troops of the interior ministry and they in fact knew everything about me. Finally I ended up in the labor camp in Workuta…"

SS-Obergruppenführer Pfeffer-Wildenbruch commanded the VI SS Volunteer Army Corps (Latvian) from 8/10/1943 until 1/7/1944. In 1945 he was awarded the Knight's Cross and the Oak Leaves for his role in the defense of Budapest.

SS-Gruppenführer von Treuenfeld was a complete failure as commander of the VI SS Volunteer Army Corps and was relieved after just three weeks.

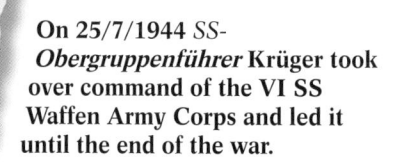

On 25/7/1944 *SS-Obergruppenführer* Krüger took over command of the VI SS Waffen Army Corps and led it until the end of the war.

Appendix
The VI SS Waffen Army Corps (Latvian)

Headquarters, VI SS Volunteer Army Corps was established at Training Camp Grafenwöhr on 8 October 1943 to command the 15th Latvian SS Volunteer Division and the 2nd Latvian SS Volunteer Brigade. Initially deployed separately, at the end of February 1944 the two units were combined under the new corps headquarters in the "Panther Position".

The two divisions[48] were deployed together under the corps headquarters until the end of July 1944. In the summer of 1944 it was renamed VI SS Waffen Army Corps (Latvian). Badly battered during the Soviet summer offensive, the remnants of the 15th SS Waffen Grenadier Division (Latvian No.2) left the corps and were sent to Germany to reform.

Until the end of the war the VI SS Waffen Army Corps (Latvian) commanded army units as well as the 19th SS Waffen Grenadier Division (Latvian No.2) and surrendered to the Red Army in Courland.

Commanding Generals

08/10/1943 - 01/07/1944 *SS-Obergruppenführer* Karl Pfeffer-Wildenbruch
Karl Pfeffer-Wildenbruch was born in Rüdersdorf near Berlin on 12 June 1888. After completing school, on 7 March 1907 he joined Field Artillery Regiment 22 as an officer candidate. On 1 August 1908 he was promoted to *Leutnant*. During the First World War he served on the staff of the German military mission in Constantinople and with the 11th Infantry Division. He joined the Schutz*polizei* in August 1919 and also served as a consultant in the Reich Ministry of the Interior. In 1933 *Oberstleutnant* Pfeffer-Wildenbruch was placed in command of a Landes*polizei* regiment and in May 1936 he was named Inspector General of Police Schools. On 1 May 1937 he was promoted to *Generalmajor der Polizei*. Pfeffer-Wildenbruch joined the Allgemeine-SS on 12 March 1939 and was made commander of the Police Division. He was then promoted to *SS-Brigadeführer* with an effective date of 20 April 1940. From 1941 to autumn 1943 he served as head of the Colonial Police Office and on 8 October 1943 took over the VI SS Volunteer Army Corps (Latvian). On 9 November Pfeffer-Wildenbruch was promoted to the rank of *SS-Obergruppenführer* and *General der Waffen-SS und Polizei*. After the successful withdrawal to the "Panther Position", he relinquished command of the corps to *SS-Gruppenführer* von Treuenfeld. At the beginning of December 1944 he took over command of the IX SS Waffen Mountain Corps in Budapest. On 11 January 1945 he was awarded the Knight's Cross of the Iron Cross for the defense of the Hungarian capital and on 1 February 1945 received the Knight's Cross with Oak Leaves. He was captured by the Soviets on 11 February 1945 and was not released until October 1955. Pfeffer-Wildenbruch died in Bielefeld on 29 January 1971.

01/07/1944 - 24/07/1944 *SS-Gruppenführer* Karl von Treuenfeld
Karl von Treuenfeld was born in Flensburg on 31 March 1885 and in 1903 he joined the 4th Guards Field Artillery Regiment Potsdam as an officer candidate. Promoted to *Leutnant* in 1904, he took part in the First World War and in 1920 was discharged from active service. Until 1939 he worked in private enterprise and in April of that year he joined the SS with the rank of *SS-Oberführer*. From 2 December 1939 to 24 April 1941 he was inspector of SS Officer Schools and then commanded the 2nd SS Motorized Brigade until 4 July 1941.

---

48 By then the 2nd Latvian SS Volunteer Brigade had been reorganized as the 19th SS Volunteer Division (Latvian No. 2).

Relieved after fierce criticism of his command style, he subsequently held the posts of SS Commander "Northeast", "Northwest" and "Bohemia Moravia" in succession. In the latter position (1 December 1941 to 26 August 1942) he was responsible for apprehending Heydrich's killers, who on 18 June 1942 were hiding in a church in Prague. After further differences, at the end of 1942 he was transferred to the position of Commander of the Waffen-SS "Russia South and Ukraine". Then in mid-November 1943 he took over formation of the 10th SS Panzer Division *"Frundsberg"*. On 30 January 1944 he was named *SS-Gruppenführer* and *Generalleutnant der Waffen-SS*. As soon as the division saw action, it became obvious that von Treuenfeld was not capable of commanding a panzer division. He was therefore relieved on 22 April 1944, but because of a lack of alternatives he was placed in command of VI SS Volunteer Army Corps (Latvian) on 1 July 1944. His orders created an extremely critical situation and on 25 July 1944 he was again relieved of command. The former commanding general of an army corps was subsequently named Inspector of Motorized Troops in the Waffen-SS. On 6 January 1945 he was released from this position and transferred to the officer reserve. Captured by the Americans, on 6 June 1946 von Treuenfeld committed suicide in Allendorf near Wetzlar.

25/07/1944 - 09/05/1945 *SS-Obergruppenführer* Walther Krüger

Walther Krüger was born in Strassburg on 27 February 1890, and after attending cadet institutes in Karlsruhe and Berlin-Lichterfelde he was promoted to *Leutnant* in the 2nd Baden Grenadier Regiment 110 in 1908. During the First World War he saw action in the west, Tyrol and Serbia as a *Hauptmann* and battalion commander. In 1919 he served in a *Freikorps* in the Baltic States. After serving briefly in the *Reichswehr*, Krüger then went into private enterprise. In 1934 he joined the office of the SA "Commander of Training" (Chef AW), which was commanded by his brother Wilhelm Krüger. After the SA was disbanded in the spring of 1935, he joined the *SS-Verfügungstruppe* and subsequently commanded II Battalion of the *SS-Standarte "Germania"* with the rank of *SS-Obersturmbannführer*. After a stint as an instructor at the SS officer school in Bad Tölz, Krüger, an *SS-Standartenführer* since 30 January 1939, was named operations officer during formation of the *Polizei-Division*. Named *SS-Brigadeführer* on 20 April 1941, from 25 May to 25 June 1941 he commanded the 1st SS Motorized Infantry Brigade. This was followed in August 1941 by command of the SS *Polizei-Division*, for which he was decorated with the Knight's Cross of the Iron Cross on 13 December 1941. After a secondment to the Inspector of Infantry in SS Headquarters, on 30 January 1942 Krüger was promoted to *SS-Gruppenführer*. On 3 April 1943 he assumed command of the 2nd SS Panzer Division *"Das Reich"* and on 31 August was awarded the Oak Leaves. From autumn 1943 to 14 March 1944 he took over Headquarters, IV SS Panzer Corps and subsequently acted as Commander of the Waffen-SS in *"Ostland"*. Promoted to *SS-Obergruppenführer* on 21 June 1944, on 24 July 1944 he took over VI SS Volunteer Army Corps (Latvian), part of Army Group North. While commanding general, on 1 February 1945 Krüger was awarded the Knight's Cross with Oak Leaves and Swords. After the surrender he tried to make his way to Germany. On 22 May 1945 he was caught by Soviet troops and committed suicide.

MILITARY POSTAL NUMBERS

Corps Headquarters	01 800
SS Corps Artillery Battalion 106	10 887
SS Corps Signals Battalion 106	11 579
SS Corps Supply Battalion 106	04 793
SS Military Police Company 106	59 973
SS Flak Battery 106	20 258
SS Field Hospital 106	10 749
SS Field Post Office 106	15 360

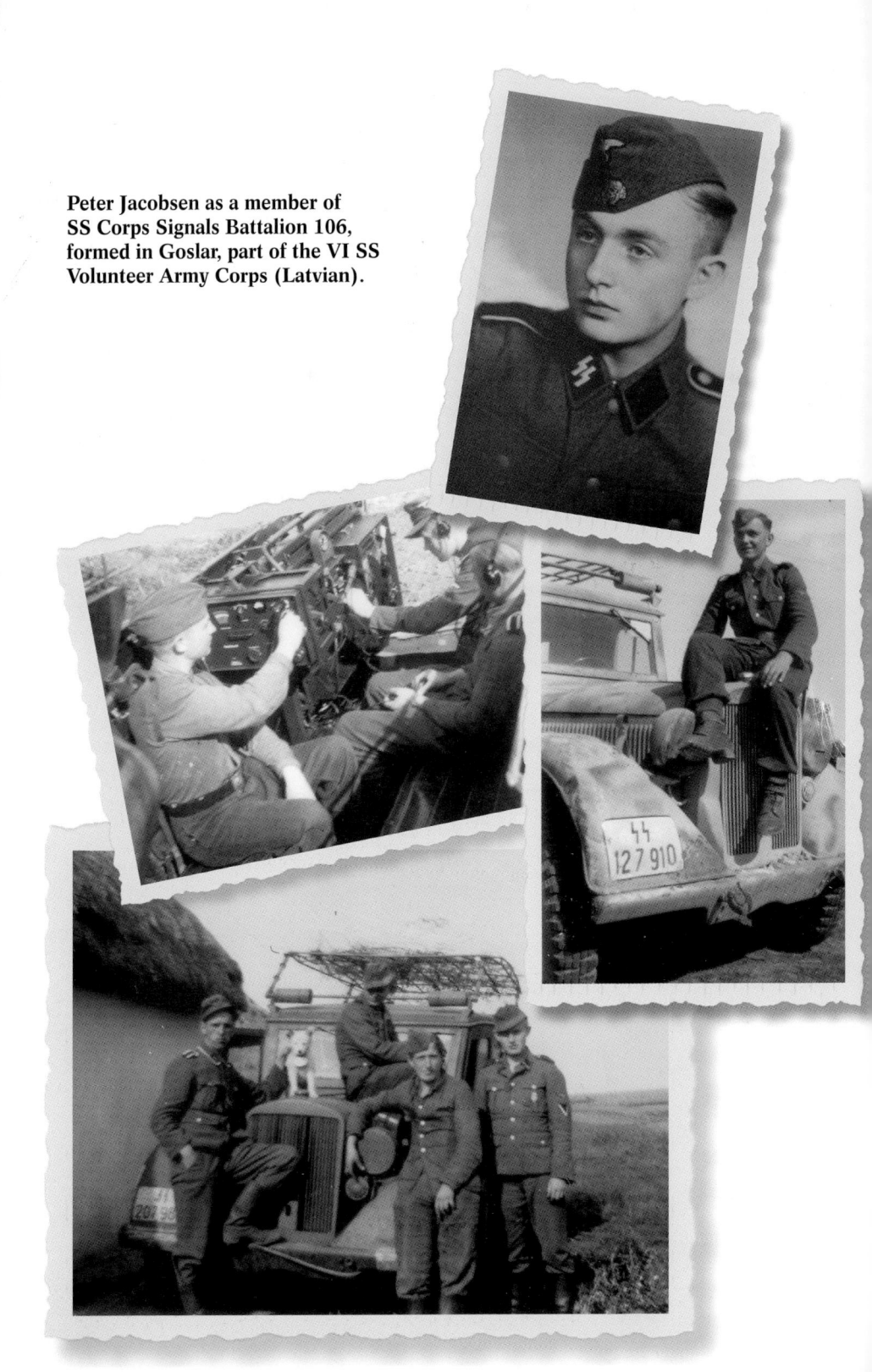

Peter Jacobsen as a member of SS Corps Signals Battalion 106, formed in Goslar, part of the VI SS Volunteer Army Corps (Latvian).

The Latvian Field Replacement Depot

After the collapse of the Eastern Front in the summer of 1944, thousands of Latvians in German service were evacuated to Germany. The main reason for this was to secure the manpower potential that could not be reorganized and refurbished in Latvia on account of the military situation. As well, the German leadership feared that the Latvians would desert from their units at home. It had not forgotten the mass flights by members of the 15th SS Waffen Grenadier Division (Latvian No.1) in July 1944.

While the members of the first Latvian division remained together within the framework of a large unit for reorganization in Germany, the remnants of many Latvian police battalions and regiments were located in West Prussia. In order to ensure uniform command and reorganization, on 28 November 1944 SS Operational Headquarters ordered the formation of a Latvian Field Replacement Depot[49]. Under the command of *SS-Oberführer* Martin, seconded from the 10th SS Panzer Division *"Frundsberg"*, the depot was supposed to have the organization of an Infantry Division 44. The SS Grenadier Training and Replacement Battalion of the 15th SS Waffen Grenadier Division (Latvian No.1) in Berent was attached to the Latvian Field Replacement Depot effective 1 December 1944, however it retained its original designation.

Of the approximately 87,000 Latvians in German service (on 1 July 1944), about 30,000 were evacuated to Germany by the end of 1944. Approximately 19,000 were used to reform the 15th SS Waffen Grenadier Division (Latvian No.1) and the SS Grenadier Training and Replacement Battalion. The remaining 11,000 were attached to the Latvian Field Replacement Depot. While the depot was supposed to be organized on the lines of an Infantry Division 44, in fact its only similarity was the same number of battalions. Instead of three grenadier regiments of two battalions plus an artillery regiment with four battalions and five combat support battalions, three (construction) regiments of five battalions each were formed and given the Roman numerals I-XV.

The Latvian Field Replacement Depot was initially assigned to construct positions in the Hammerstein area, and at the end of February it moved to Stettin, partly on foot and partly by rail. The arriving depot members, most of whom were from police units, were not used in a combat role again. Instead they were employed as construction pioneers. The reason for this was the inability to provide the unit with the necessary weapons and the fact that most of the men were no longer fit for combat.[50]

On 1 March 1945 the depot, not counting SS Grenadier Training and Replacement Battalion 15, had an actual strength of:

	Officers	NCOs	Enlisted Men	Total
Latvians	360	2,077	8,166	10,603
	3.0%	14.1%	82.9%	100%
Germans	29	31	38	98

---

49 Interestingly, there was no talk of a Latvian SS Field Replacement Depot. The reason for this is that the depot was established primarily as a collection point for Latvian members of the police and SS border defense regiments evacuated to Germany.
50 Men from older age classes and some not entirely fit for frontline military service were also inducted into the Latvian volunteer police and SS border defense regiments.

Instead of the Sigrunen, members of the 2nd Latvian SS Volunteer Brigade and later the 19th Latvian SS Volunteer Division were supposed to wear the Latvian ugunskrusts (fire cross/swastika) on their right collar patch. In fact, most wore the Sigrunen. In the photo below, *SS-Sturmbannführer* Koop is wearing the special version for officers.

From left to right: *SS-Sturmbannführer* Koop (operations officer of the 19th SS Waffen Grenadier Division (Latvian No.2)), *Waffen-Standartenführer* Skaistlaukis (C.O. SS Waffen Artillery Regiment 15), *SS-Gruppenführer* Bangerskis (Inspector of the Latvian SS Volunteer Legion), *SS-Brigadeführer* Streckenbach (C.O. of the 19th SS Waffen Grenadier Division (Latvian No.2)), and *Waffen-Oberführer* Silgailis (Chief-of-Staff/Inspector of the Latvian SS Volunteer Legion).

On 12 March 1945 a regiment was put together under the command of *Waffen-Obersturmbannführer* Rusmanis and shipped to Courland, where it was attached to VI SS Waffen Army Corps (Latvian).

The remaining elements of the Latvian Field Replacement Depot moved to Neubrandenburg and from there marched into captivity in the hands of the western allies.

Command Positions

Commanding Officer, *SS-Oberführer* Georg Martin
Georg Martin was born on 26 September 1897 and joined the NSDAP (membership number 5 649 799) and the SS (87 679). From 17 August 1936 to 1 June 1939 he commanded the 72. *SS-Standarte Lippe* (headquarters in Detmold) with the rank of *SS-Sturmbannführer*. On 11 November 1939 *SS-Obersturmbannführer* Martin was placed in command of III Battalion, *SS-Totenkopf-Standarte 7*. From the beginning of April until the end of July 1940 Martin commanded *SS-Totenkopf-Standarte 14*. After promotion to *SS-Oberführer*, from the summer of 1941 to 20 March 1942 he commanded the SS Driving School in Vienna. After serving as quartermaster in the headquarters of the 10th SS Panzer Division *"Frundsberg"*, in November 1944 he took command of the Latvian Field Replacement Depot. Martin is believed to have committed suicide on 9 May 1945.

Commander 1st (Construction) Regiment   *Waffen-Standartenführer* Veckalnins
Reinholds Veckalnins was born in Skujene (Latvia) on 20 April 1896 and in 1915 joined the Latvian Army. In 1934 he achieved the rank of light colonel and for a time was the military attaché in Finland and Estonia. In the Latvian SS Volunteer Brigade he served as quartermaster (I b) and in autumn 1944 took over the 1st Regiment in the Latvian Field Replacement Depot. After the war Veckalnins emigrated to Canada and died in Montreal on 24 March 1981.

Commander 2nd (Construction) Regiment
Waffen-Obersturmbannführer Janis Grosbergs
Janis Grosbergs was born in Rujina on 28 August 1896 and attended the Russian Military Academy in Irkutsk. From June 1916 to December 1917 he was a member of the Latvian 5th Rifle Regiment, and after the First World War he remained in military service as a lieutenant. Promoted to light colonel in 1925, until 1940 he served in the XXIV Soviet Rifle Corps. In 1943 Grosbergs joined the Latvian SS Volunteer Legion as a *Legions-Obersturmbannführer*, and in the summer of 1944 he commanded Latvian Volunteer Police Regiment 2. He led the 2nd Regiment until the end of September 1944. After the war he emigrated to Canada and died in St. John's (Newfoundland) on 29 April 1970.

Waffen-Obersturmbannführer Nikolajs Rusmanis
Nikolajs Rusmanis was born in Latvia on 13 February 1895 and served in the Latvian Army, ultimately as a lieutenant-colonel, until 17 June 1940. He was taken into the Latvian SS Legion with the same rank (*Oberstleutnant*) and initially commanded Latvian Volunteer Police Regiment 3. Evacuated to Germany, at the beginning of October 1944 he took over the 2nd Regiment. In March 1945 a regiment-strength battle group was formed under his command and transported from Germany to Latvia by sea. Rusmanis was sentenced to death by Stalin on 6 January 1946 and was executed soon after.

Commander 3rd (Construction) Regiment, *Waffen-Standartenführer* Teodors Brigge
Teodors Brigge was born in Latvia on 6 October 1891. Until August 1944 he commanded Latvian SS Border Defense Regiment 6. After evacuation to Germany, in autumn 1944 he took over command of the Latvian Field Replacement Depot's 3rd Regiment. He died on 20 November 1970.

Division Commanders
15th SS Waffen Grenadier Division (Latvian No.1)

The commanders of the first Latvian SS division show that the Waffen-SS was suffering from a shortage of capable generals. *SS-Brigadeführer* Hansen, commander of the formation staff, was not replaced by *SS-Brigadeführer* Pückler-Burghaus until the end of the first three-month formation phase. Pückler-Burghaus had no experience in commanding a combat unit and he showed himself to be beyond his depth when the unit took over its own sector in the main line of resistance. With a Soviet offensive imminent, he was replaced by *SS-Oberführer* Heilmann, who, during the chaotic retreat that followed, enforced iron discipline in an effort to maintain control of his disintegrating unit. He had a number of Latvians court-martialed and shot for losing their weapons, whereupon Himmler immediately had him relieved. Attached to the 23rd Infantry Division and then the 19th SS Waffen Grenadier Division (Latvian No.2), the division was subsequently led on an interim basis by *SS-Oberführer* von Obwurzer (C.O. of Latvian SS Grenadier Training and Replacement Brigade 15). In the existing situation he was the most expedient solution, even though he had lost Himmler's trust after his failure as commander of the 13th Croatian SS Volunteer Division. Four months later, when the division was ordered into action, von Obwurzer was killed on the first day. He was replaced for four weeks by *SS-Oberführer* Ax, who since the spring of 1942 had only served in occupied Holland. Undoubtedly capable of commanding smaller units, Ax was overtaxed by the command of a division. The division's last commanding officer, *SS-Brigadeführer* Burk, had more administrative than tactical experience. He was the de facto chief-of-staff of the 5th SS Volunteer Assault Brigade *"Wallonien"* (as an *SS-Brigadeführer* sic!) and served as the connecting link between the German command and the Wallonian brigade commander.

25/02/1943 - 17/05/1943 *SS-Brigadeführer* **Hansen**
Peter Hansen was born in Santiago de Chile on 30 November 1896, and after completing school in Dresden he joined the 4th Royal Saxon Field Artillery Regiment No. 48 as an officer candidate on 1 September 1914. Promoted to *Leutnant* in 1916, after the First World War he saw action in a *Freikorps*. Hansen then briefly served in the *Reichswehr* as an *Oberleutnant*. He then returned to Chile but moved back to Germany in 1933. With the rank of *SS-Obersturmbannführer* he was a member of *SS-Oberabschnitt* "Mitte" until August 1935. That year he rejoined the military and was made commander of Artillery Battalion 50 with the rank of Major. On 1 June 1939 he transferred to the *SS-Verfügungstruppe* and commanded the *SS-Artillerie-Standarte* (*SS-Standartenführer* since 19 October 1939). On 13 December 1940, while holding the same position, he was promoted to *SS-Oberführer*. In October 1941 he joined the SS-FHA as Artillery Inspector. On 30 January 1942 he was promoted to *SS-Brigadeführer*. On 10 April 1942 his office was renamed 4th Inspectorate (Artillery and Flak) of the SS Operational Headquarters' Department Group C. From 25 February to 17 May 1943 he took over the task of commander of the formation staff of the 15th Latvian SS Volunteer Division. After the initial formation phase ended,, on 2 October 1943 he took over the Italian *Milizia Armata*, which was attached to the *Ordnungspolizei*, not least because of his good knowledge of Italian. On 10 July 1944 he received another artillery command, becoming Arko (artillery commander) of the III (Germanic) SS Panzer Corps. In November 1944 he took over the same position with I SS Panzer Corps and on 5 February 1945 was named chief-of-staff in XVIII SS Army Corps. Hansen died in Viersen on 23 May 1967.

17/05/1943 - 16/02/1944 *SS-Brigadeführer* **Pückler-Burghaus**
Pückler-Burghaus was born in Friedland (Silesia) on 7 October 1886 and from 1905 to 1908 studied law and political science in Bonn and Breslau. On 1 April 1908 he joined

the Bodyguard Cuirassier Regiment *"Großer Kurfürst"* (Silesian) No. 1 and on 18 October 1907 received his *Leutnant's* commission. He served in the general staff during the First World War and in September 1919 began working on his parents' estates. He joined the NSDAP on 1 December 1931 and became a member of the SA. On 10 April 1933 he was promoted to *SA-Oberführer*. On 1 July 1934, following the Röhm putsch, Pückler-Burghaus, who was working in SA headquarters, temporarily left the organization and resumed his activities as estate manager until the beginning of 1937. Promoted to *SA-Brigadeführer* on 1 May 1937, on 1 July 1940 he was taken into the SS with the rank of *SS-Brigadeführer*. At the beginning of 1942 he was named deputy to the Senior SS and Police Commander "Russia Center" and on 12 September 1942 was assigned to the Protectorate of Bohemia Moravia as commander of the Waffen-SS. In May 1943 he oversaw the final phase of the formation of the 15th Latvian SS Volunteer Division with the rank of *SS-Gruppenführer* and *Generalleutnant der Waffen-SS*. Pückler-Burghaus proved unfit to command the division on the Eastern Front and on 17 February 1944 he was relieved of command and reassigned to his former position. When the Prague uprising broke out in May 1945, Pückler-Burghaus planned to use the Luftwaffe to destroy the city, but by then the air force was incapable of such an operation. Captured by the Americans, he committed suicide on 13 May 1945 rather than be handed over to the Czechs. He was buried in the central cemetery in Berlin.

17/02/1944 - 21/07/1944 *SS-Oberführer* Heilmann

Nikolaus Heilmann was born in Grundlhelm (Hesse) on 20 April 1903 and on 1 April 1925 entered the police service. On 1 April 1930 he was promoted to *Leutnant* der Schupo and on 1 April 1932 to *Oberleutnant der Schupo*. He taught tactics and other subjects at the Berlin Police School and in May 1939 joined the SS with the rank of *SS-Hauptsturmführer*. When the *Polizei-Division* was formed he initially served as adjutant in Police Infantry Regiment 3 and finally, from 16 September 1940 to 4 April 1943 as Operations Officer in the *SS-Polizei-Division*. On 20 April 1941 Heilmann was promoted to *SS-Sturmbannführer* and *Major der Schupo* and on 5 January 1942 to *SS-Obersturmbannführer* and *Oberstleutnant der Schupo*. Decorated with the German Cross in Gold on 12 August 1942, Heilmann was transferred to the SS Panzer Grenadier Division *"Das Reich"*. Following promotion to *SS-Standartenführer* on 21 June 1943, he served as Operations Officer in Headquarters, IV SS Panzer Corps, which was later renamed VI SS Volunteer Army Corps (Latvian). On 17 February 1944 *SS-Oberführer* Heilmann took over as commander of the 15th Latvian SS Volunteer Division, a position he held until he had members of the division shot for losing their weapons (sic!). Beginning 20 July 1944, he led the IV SS Panzer Corps in an acting capacity for 16 days, and on 23 August he was awarded the Knight's Cross of the Iron Cross retroactively for his firm command of the 15th SS Waffen Grenadier Division (sic!). From 12 December 1944 to 30 January 1945 Heilmann commanded the 28th SS Volunteer Grenadier Division *"Wallonien"* and was then supposed to take over general command of XXI Army Corps in an acting capacity[51]. On 29 January 1945, while on the way there, Heilmann was killed in Mittwalde (SW of Schwiebus). He was promoted to *SS-Brigadeführer* posthumously with the promotion backdated to the day of his death.

21/07/1944 - 26/01/1945 *SS-Oberführer* von Obwurzer

Herbert von Obwurzer was born in Innsbruck on 23 June 1888 and after leaving secondary school in Vienna he joined the military. He served as a *Leutnant* in the

---

[51] The commanding general, General der Artillerie Petzel, had been relieved by Himmler on 29 January 1945. Heilmann was supposed to take over general command of the corps.

Dragoon Regiment "Kaiser Ferdinand I" and fought in the First World War, ultimately with the rank of *Hauptmann*. In 1920 he served with the Iron Division, which fought against the Red Army in Latvia. In 1930 he became a member of the NSDAP in Austria, but in the same year he resettled in Germany. In 1937 von Obwurzer took part in exercises with Infantry Regiment 67 and two years later saw action in the Polish campaign as a *Major* with the same unit. He subsequently took over the II Battalion of Infantry Regiment 411 and saw action in Russia. By then an *Oberstleutnant der Reserve*, on 1 August 1942 von Obwurzer joined the Waffen-SS as an *SS-Obersturmbannführer der Reserve*. Following promotion to *SS-Standartenführer* on 30 January 1943, from 12 March until 8 September he commanded the 13th Croatian SS Volunteer Division. In this position von Obwurzer demonstrated that he had absolutely no desire to lead a division made up of foreign volunteers. An attempt to give him command of the 1st SS Motorized Infantry Brigade also failed. He was relieved of command on 18 October 1943, after just four weeks. Having shown himself to be completely ill suited to command a combat unit, in mid-March 1944 von Obwurzer was named commander of SS Grenadier Training and Replacement Brigade 15. After Himmler decided that Heilmann, commander of the 15th SS Waffen Grenadier Division, should be relieved as soon as possible, on 21 July 1944 von Obwurzer was named commander of the division and simultaneously promoted to *SS-Oberführer*. As plans called for the division to be reformed in Germany, von Obwurzer initially held the position in name only. Elements of the division were subsequently rushed into action and on 26 January 1945 von Obwurzer was killed while driving to the front. Initially reported missing near Altlinden, it turned out he had been killed. Despite his unmotivated service, von Obwurzer was promoted by Himmler to the rank of *SS-Brigadeführer* posthumously.

26/01/1945 - 15/02/1945 *SS-Oberführer* Ax

Adolf Ax was born in Mouscron, Belgium on 23 June 1906 and in 1930 he joined the NSDAP and the SS. In 1939, as an *SS-Hauptsturmführer*, he led the *SS-Verfügungs-Division's* anti-tank battalion. After promotion to *SS-Sturmbannführer* on 25 April 1940, in December Ax transferred to III Battalion, SS Motorized Infantry Regiment 11. He subsequently attended various unit leader courses, including one at the *Panzertruppenschule* in Wünsdorf. From December 1941 to March 1942 he was in Berlin due to health problems. After convalescence, on 18 July 1942 he took over the SS Anti-Tank Training and Replacement Battalion in Hilversum (Netherlands). Ax subsequently served as Operations Officer under the Commander of the Waffen-SS "Netherlands". He was later named Chief-of-Staff to the Commander of the Waffen-SS "Netherlands" and promoted to the rank of *SS-Standartenführer*. In November 1944 he served as Chief-of-Staff in Operations Staff "East Coast" and on 21 December 1944 was promoted to *SS-Oberführer*. After Operations Staff "East Coast" was used to form the corps headquarters of the XVI SS Army Corps, from 15 January 1945 Ax functioned as its chief-of-staff. The corps was short-lived, however. On 26 January 1945 Ax was placed in command of the 15th SS Waffen Grenadier Division (Latvian No.1) and the XVIII Mountain Corps assumed command of the units in that area. Ax was relieved of command of the Latvians in mid-February 1945 and placed in command of the 32nd SS Volunteer Grenadier Division "30 January" on the Oder front. This command was also short-lived. In March 1945 he began a course for senior commanders in Bad Wiessee. Ax died in Wiesbaden on 6 February 1983.

15/02/1945 - 09/05/1945 *SS-Oberführer* Burk

Karl Burk was born in Buchenau, Bavaria on 14 March 1898. He joined the Lower Saxon Infantry Regiment 155 in 1916 and saw action during the First World War. After the war he stayed in the 100,000-man army and served until 1927 as an Ober*wachtmeister* in Foot Artillery Regiment 10. On 1 March 1933 he joined the SS with the rank of *SS-Oberscharführer* and worked in *SS-Oberabschnitt "Südost"* until 1941. From 9 January 1939 to 1 March 1941 Burk, ultimately as an *SS-Standartenführer*, commanded the 8. *SS-Standarte* in Hirschberg (Silesia). After serving briefly in the SS Artillery Regiment *"Wiking"*, on 1 May 1941 he took over SS Flak Battalion *"Ost"*. In the fighting at the Volkhov he commanded a mixed battle group and on 15 November 1942 was awarded the German Cross in Gold for his actions. Following promotion to *SS-Oberführer* on 9 November 1943, he took over command of the SS Flak Training and Replacement Regiment. On 21 December 1944 he took charge of the headquarters of the 5th SS Volunteer Assault Brigade *"Wallonien"*, which subsequently formed the basis of the 28th SS Volunteer Grenadier Division *"Wallonien"*. Burk was transferred to the officer reserve on 12 December 1944 and on 15 February 1945 took over the 15th SS Waffen Grenadier Division (Latvian No.1), which he commanded until the end of the war. He was promoted to *SS-Brigadeführer* on 20 April 1945. Burk died in Fritzlar (Hesse) on 23 September 1963.

19TH SS WAFFEN GRENADIER DIVISION (LATVIAN NO.2)

In contrast to the first Latvian SS volunteer division, the second was commanded by officers with frontline experience.

18/05/1943 - 04/09/1943 *SS-Brigadeführer* von Scholz

Friedrich Max Karl von Scholz was born on 9 December 1896 in Pilsen. After completing high school he joined the Imperial Austro-Hungarian Army in August 1914. Transferred from Field Cannon Regiment 22 to Field Howitzer Regiment 3, he rose to the rank of *Leutnant*. He was subsequently transferred to Field Artillery Regiment 40 as signals officer and later to Field Artillery Regiment 125. There he was promoted to *Oberleutnant* in November 1917. After the war he initially served in *Freikorps "Oberland"*, after which he worked as a chemical engineer in southern Germany and Austria. On 9 October 1932 von Scholz joined the Austrian Nazi Party. After serving briefly in the SA, in June 1933 he joined the SS and served in the Austrian SS Legion. On 1 February 1934 he became the Legion's adjutant and on 21 August 1934 was promoted to *SS-Untersturmführer*. After promotion to *SS-Obersturmführer* on 30 January 1935, on 11 April he was given command of the 5th Company, *SS-Standarte 1* of the *SS-Verfügungstruppe*. One year later von Scholz was promoted to *SS-Hauptsturmführer*. On 1 April 1938 *SS-Sturmbannführer* von Scholz was placed in command of II Battalion, *SS-Standarte 3*, and on 30 January 1940 he was promoted to *SS-Obersturmbannführer*. On 1 December 1940 he took over the SS Regiment *"Nordland"*. He was promoted to *SS-Standartenführer* on 30 January 1941 and to *SS-Oberführer* on 1 October. On 22 November 1941 von Scholz was decorated with the German Cross in Gold and on 19 January 1942 received the Knight's Cross. Following promotion to *SS-Brigadeführer* and *Generalmajor der Waffen-SS* on 21 December 1942, in January 1943 he briefly took over the 1st SS Motorized Infantry Brigade, replacing *SS-Brigadeführer* Treuenfeld who had been relieved of command. On 23 January 1943 von Scholz was named commander of the 2nd SS Motorized Infantry Brigade for several weeks. Effective 1 May 1943 von Scholz was appointed commander of SS Panzer Grenadier Division *"Nordland"*. During formation of the unit, however, he was called away to temporarily lead the Latvian SS Volunteer Brigade at the Volkhov. In September 1943 he returned to his previous command, and on 12 March 1944 he was awarded the Knight's Cross with Oak Leaves. On 20 April von Scholz was promoted to *SS-Gruppenführer* and *Generalleutnant der Waffen-SS*. On 27 July 1944 von Scholz was badly wounded and died in hospital the next day. On 8 August 1944 Hitler awarded him the Knight's Cross with Swords and Oak Leaves posthumously.

05/09/1943 - 15/03/1944 *SS-Brigadeführer* Schuldt
Hinrich Schuldt was born in Hamburg on 14 January 1901. At the age of 21 he entered the *Reichsmarine* as an officer candidate and in 1926 was promoted to *Leutnant* zur *See*. In 1933 he transferred to the SS and joined the *SS-Leibstandarte "Adolf Hitler"*, where he led the 3rd (Assault) Company. In March 1935 Schuldt achieved the rank of *SS-Hauptsturmführer* and in the spring of 1938 took over the 1st Battalion of *SS-Standarte "Deutschland"* as an *SS-Sturmbannführer*. From 5 July 1941 he commanded SS Motorized Infantry Regiment 4. Schuldt was promoted to *SS-Obersturmführer* on 1 September 1941. Schuldt, who according to personal files was once thought of as a "queer" by Himmler, was awarded the Knight's Cross on 5 April 1942. Four months later, on 1 August 1942, he was promoted to *SS-Standartenführer*. From the beginning of December 1942 until March 1943 Schuldt commanded a battle group on the Don front, and in recognition of his actions on 2 April 1943 he became the 220th soldier to receive the Knight's Cross with Oak Leaves. At the beginning of September 1943 Schuldt took over the Latvian SS Volunteer Brigade, which in the spring of 1944 was expanded into the 19th Latvian SS Volunteer Division. On 15 March 1944, Schuldt was killed near Ostrov. He was buried in the cemetery at the cathedral in Riga (Archibiska Cathedral). Schuldt was promoted to *SS-Brigadeführer* and *Generalmajor der Waffen-SS* posthumously and on 25 March 1944 also became the 56th recipient of the Knight's Cross with Swords and Oak Leaves. A further honor was bestowed upon him when, on 15 January 1945, SS Waffen Grenadier Regiment 43 (Latvian No.2) was awarded his name, becoming SS Waffen Grenadier Regiment 43 "Hinrich Schuldt".

15/03/1944 - 26/03/1944 *SS-Standartenführer* Bock
Friedrich-Wilhelm Bock was born on 6 May 1897 in Wreschen in Wartheland. After graduating from secondary school, on 2 August 1914 he volunteered for military service and joined Field Artillery Regiment 38. At the beginning of February 1919 *Leutnant* Bock was demobilized and subsequently took part in the fighting in the Baltic as a member of a *Freikorps*. On 15 November 1922 he joined the Hamburg police as a *Wachtmeister* and in April 1926 moved to the Prussian Police in Stettin. He joined the NSDAP on 1 May 1933 and, after serving in the Hanover Police, in late summer 1939 was named commander of Police Battalion 3, which was deployed in occupied Poland. At the beginning of May 1940, by then a *Major der Schutzpolizei*, Schuldt took over the II Battalion of the Police Artillery Regiment (Police Division). On 5 January 1942 Bock was promoted to *SS-Obersturmbannführer* and *Oberstleutnant der Schutzpolizei* and on 28 March 1943 was awarded the Knight's Cross. Bock assumed command of the regiment on 1 August 1943 and on 9 November was promoted to *SS-Standartenführer*. He subsequently commanded the remnants of the SS Police Division until he assumed command of the 19th Latvian SS Volunteer Division on 15 March 1944. After he was replaced by *SS-Oberführer* Streckenbach, Bock was initially transferred to the officer reserve. At the beginning of June 1944 he became artillery commander of the II SS Panzer Corps. Promoted to *SS-Oberführer* on 1 August 1944, he subsequently took command of the 9th SS Panzer Division *"Hohenstaufen"*. On 2 September 1944 Bock was awarded the Knight's Cross with Oak Leaves for his command accomplishments. On 10 October 1944 he again took over the position of corps artillery commander of the II SS Panzer Corps. Bock died in Hanover on 11 March 1978.

26/03/1944 - 09/05/1945 *SS-Gruppenführer* Streckenbach
Bruno Streckenbach was born in Hamburg on 7 February 1902 and in 1920 be began an apprenticeship with a Hamburg import firm. He subsequently worked in a number of fields, including as a foreign language correspondent with ADAC and the Norddeutschen Rundfunk. On 1 December 1930 Streckenbach joined the NSDAP and on 1 September 1931 the SS, where two years later he reached the rank of *SS-Sturmbannführer*. On 20 October 1933 he was placed in charge of the political police in

SS-Brigadeführer Hansen commanded the formation staff of the Latvian SS Volunteer Division from 25/02 to 17/05/1943.

SS-Brigadeführer Pückler-Burghaus (center) was in command of the 15th Latvian SS Volunteer Division when it saw its first action. Overwhelmed, he was relieved on 17/02/44.

SS-Oberführer Heilmann commanded the division from 17/02 to 21/07/1944. He was relieved immediately after he had Latvian grenadiers court-martialed and shot.

SS-Oberführer Ax was charged with the command of the 15th SS Waffen Grenadier Division (Latvian No. 1) from 26/01 to 15/02/1945.

Hamburg and on 9 November was promoted to *SS-Obersturmbannführer*. Five years later Streckenbach was assigned to Defense District X as Inspector of the Security Police and SD. He was simultaneously named Government Director and promoted to *SS-Standartenführer*. On 20 April 1939 he was promoted to *SS-Brigadeführer*. After

SS-Brigadeführer von Scholz was envisaged as commander of the 11th SS Volunteer Panzer Grenadier Division "Nordland", however during the unit's formation he commanded the Latvian SS Volunteer Brigade at the Volkhov from 18 May to 4 September 1943.

SS-Standartenführer Schuldt took over on 5/9/1943 and commanded the unit until his death on 15/3/1944.

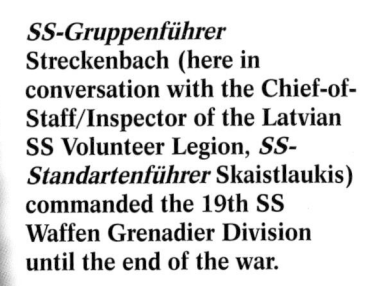

SS-Gruppenführer Streckenbach (here in conversation with the Chief-of-Staff/Inspector of the Latvian SS Volunteer Legion, *SS-Standartenführer* Skaistlaukis) commanded the 19th SS Waffen Grenadier Division until the end of the war.

the campaign against Poland he was made commander of the Security Police and SD in the Generalgouvernement. There he ordered the shooting of about 8,000 Polish intellectuals and criminals who were *"needlessly filling the jails"*. In January 1941 he took over Department I in the Reich Central Security Office and was simultaneously promoted to *SS-Brigadeführer* and *Generalmajor der Polizei*. That same year, on 9 November, he was promoted to *SS-Gruppenführer* and *Generalleutnant der Polizei*. On 14 December 1942 he appealed personally to Himmler for permission to serve at the front. He subsequently joined the Waffen-SS as an *SS-Untersturmführer* and began training at the SS Anti-Tank Training and Replacement Battalion in Holland. In March 1943 he was promoted to *SS-Sturmbannführer der Reserve (Waffen-SS)* and named commander of the SS Cavalry Division's anti-tank battalion. On 15 December 1943 he was awarded the German Cross in Gold for repeated acts of bravery. After completing a course at the armored forces school in Wünsdorf, Streckenbach was promoted to *SS-Oberführer* and placed in command of the SS Cavalry Division. On 26 March 1944 he took over the 19th Latvian SS Volunteer Division and on 1 July was promoted to *SS-Brigadeführer* and *Generalmajor der Waffen-SS*. On 27 August 1944 Streckenbach was decorated with the Knight's Cross of the Iron Cross. Then on 9 November he was promoted to *SS-Gruppenführer* and *Generalleutnant der Waffen-SS*. On 15 January 1945 he became the 701st recipient of the Knight's Cross with Oak Leaves. Captured in Courland, Streckenbach was held as a POW until 10 October 1955, when he returned to Germany. There he worked as a salesman in Hamburg. A number of judicial inquiries were held to investigate suspected war crimes, however Streckenbach was never charged. He died in Hamburg on 28 October 1977.

MILITARY POSTAL NUMBERS

15TH SS WAFFEN GRENADIER DIVISION (LATVIAN NO.1)

Division Headquarters	34 400
SS Waffen Grenadier Regiment 32 (Latvian No.3)	32 595
I Battalion	34 636
II Battalion	35 532
III Battalion	36 426
SS Waffen Grenadier Regiment 33 (Latvian No.4)	36 982
I Battalion	37 849
II Battalion	36 099
III Battalion	66 884
SS Waffen Grenadier Regiment 34 (Latvian No.5)	39 875
I Battalion	33 171
II Battalion	32 883
III Battalion	37 168
SS Waffen Artillery Regiment 15	40 253
I Battalion	41 204
II Battalion	42 277
III Battalion	37 313
SS Pioneer Battalion 15	38 935
SS Flak Battalion 15	57 966
SS Anti-Tank Battalion 15	33 542
SS Signals Unit 15	33 857
SS Economic Battalion 15	37 617
SS Supply Unit 15	40 866

19th SS Waffen Grenadier Division (Latvian No.2)

Division Headquarters	43 500
SS Waffen Grenadier Regiment 42 (Latvian No.1)	33 595
I Battalion	45 849
II Battalion	15 205
III Battalion	42 515
SS Waffen Grenadier Regiment 43 (Latvian No.2)	34 300
I Battalion	35 118
II Battalion	36 164
III Battalion	47 278
SS Waffen Grenadier Regiment 44 (Latvian No.6)	09 015
I Battalion	58 978
II Battalion	10 217
III Battalion	08 570
SS Waffen Artillery Regiment 19 (Latvian No.2)	02 280
I Battalion	57 958
II Battalion	12 451
III Battalion	11 861
IV Battalion	06 462
SS Pioneer Battalion 19	05 818
SS Flak Battalion 19	59 824
SS Anti-Tank Battalion 19	58 680
SS Signals Unit 19	00 577
SS Fusilier Battalion 19	08 471

Recipients of Important Decorations

German Cross in Gold

15th SS Waffen Grenadier Division (Latvian No.1)

SS-Hauptsturmführer **Hans Pomrehn, 09/03/1945**
Hans Pomrehn was born in Stolp on 10 December 1912 and on 1 April 1927 joined the police service. Six years later he became a member of the NSDAP and on 8 March 1936 he moved from the police service to I Battalion, *SS-Standarte "Germania"*. After passing through the SS officer school in Brunswick, on 9 November 1936 Pomrehn was promoted to *SS-Untersturmführer*. He remained with the *SS-Standarte "Germania"* until January 1941 and then became an instructor at the SS officer school in Brunswick, where he was promoted to *SS-Obersturmführer* on 20 April 1941. Almost two years later Pomrehn returned to frontline service, joining the 15th Latvian SS Volunteer Division during its formation. On 20 April 1943 Pomrehn was promoted to *SS-Hauptsturmführer*. On 26 January 1945 he was promoted to *SS-Sturmbannführer* and placed in command of SS Fusilier Battalion 15. Pomrehn was awarded the German Cross in Gold on 9 March 1945.

19th SS Waffen Grenadier Division (Latvian No.2)

Waffen-Sturmbannführer **Nikolajs Galdins, 19/10/1944**
Nikolajs Galdins (his name also appears as Galdinsch in German records) was born in Riga on 19 February 1902 and in 1919 joined the Latvian Army. He was promoted to lieutenant

on 1 September 1924, first lieutenant three years later and captain on 1 April 1933. He served in the Latvian 4th Infantry Regiment and later in the general staff. Galdins subsequently left active service, but in October 1942 he volunteered to serve under the Germans and on 1 April 1943 was appointed *Legions-Hauptsturmführer*. In October 1943 he took over the III Battalion of SS Volunteer Grenadier Regiment 42, and on 30 January 1944 assumed command of the regiment with a simultaneous promotion to *Legions-Sturmbannführer*. On 20 September 1944 Galdins was promoted to *Waffen-Obersturmbannführer*. He was later decorated with the German Cross in Gold and the Knight's Cross. On 5 October 1945 he was shot on Stalin's order.

Waffen-Obersturmführer Visvaldis Graumanis, 06/01/1945
Visvaldis Graumanis was born on 10 October 1913 and served in the Latvian Army. When *Schutzmannschafts* Battalion 21 was formed in February 1942, Graumanis joined its 1st Company as a *Leutnant*. After moving to the Latvian SS Volunteer Legion, in the summer of 1944 he commanded II Battalion, SS Waffen Grenadier Regiment 44. In September 1944 Graumanis suffered a serious head wound. He was flown to a hospital in the Sudetenland but died there in December 1944. On 5 January 1944 he was awarded the German Cross in Gold posthumously and promoted to the rank of *Waffen-Hauptsturmführer*.

Waffen-Sturmbannführer Voldemars Gravelis, 10/03/1945
Voldemars Gravelis was born in Latvia on 5 July 1900 and later joined the Latvian Army. From 1925 to 1931 he was a member of the Latvian national soccer team. He commanded the 3rd Company of *Schutzmannschafts* Battalion 268 with the rank of *Oberleutnant*, then in the summer of 1944 he led the II Battalion of the Latvian Volunteer Police Regiment 2 with the rank of *Waffen-Hauptsturmführer*. After moving to the 19th SS Waffen Grenadier Division (Latvian No.2), he served in SS Waffen Artillery Regiment 19, becoming its commanding officer in autumn 1944. On 10 March 1945 Gravelis was awarded the German Cross in Gold and promoted to *Waffen-Obersturmbannführer*. After the war Gravelis died in a Soviet labor camp.

Waffen-Obersturmbannführer Rudolfs Kocins, 29/01/1945
Born on 15 December 1907, Rudolfs Kocins joined the Latvian Army. With the formation of *Schutzmannschafts* Battalion 16, on 4 September 1941 he was placed in command of the unit's 4th Company with the rank of Hauptmann. On 12 December, by then a Major, he took over the entire battalion. When the unit was absorbed by the Latvian SS Volunteer Legion, on 18 April 1943 Kocins was named a Legions-Sturmbann*führer* and commander of III Battalion, SS Volunteer Regiment 1. From 11 November to 16 December 1943 he led SS Volunteer Grenadier Regiment 39. On 39 January 1944 Kocins was promoted to *Waffen-Obersturmbannführer* and appointed commander of SS Waffen Grenadier Regiment 44. On 29 January 1945 he was awarded the German Cross in Gold in recognition of his command accomplishments. After the war he wrote a military-historical treatment of the battles in Vidzeme, Latgalia and Kurzeme. Kocins died on 17 April 1990.

SS-Sturmbannführer Hans Koop, 12/09/1944
Hans Koop was born on 7 September 1914 and joined the SS in 1934. In 1937-38 he passed through the SS officer school in Bad Tölz and later led a company of the *SS-Standarte "Deutschland"* as an *SS-Hauptsturmführer*. In the summer of 1943 he took over SS Volunteer Panzer Grenadier Battalion "Narva", which was made up of Estonians. On 21 June 1944 Koop was promoted to *SS-Sturmbannführer* and named First General Staff Officer (operations officer) of the 19th SS Waffen Grenadier Division. On 12 September 1944 he was awarded the German Cross in Gold for his tactical guidance.

***Waffen-Untersturmführer* Karlis Musins, 08/05/1945**
Karlis Musins was born in Latvia and served as an officer in the Latvian Army. When *Schutzmannschafts* Battalion 28 was formed on 9 March 1942, he was placed in command of its 1st Company with the rank of *Oberleutnant*. At some point he was obviously court-martialed, resulting in a demotion, for on 8 May 1945 he was a *Waffen-Untersturmführer* commanding the 4th Company of SS Waffen Grenadier Division 42. Personally brave, on the day of the surrender he was awarded the German Cross in Gold.

***Waffen-Hauptscharführer* Janis Pikelis, 08/05/1945**
Janis Pikelis was born in Latvia in 1915 and served in the Latvian Army as a non-commissioned officer. In the Latvian SS Volunteer Legion he achieved the rank of *Waffen-Untersturmführer* by 1945 and commanded a bicycle reconnaissance platoon in SS Waffen Grenadier Regiment 44. He was awarded the German Cross in Gold on 8 May 1945.

***Waffen-Hauptsturmführer* Gustavs Praudins, 16/01/1945**
Gustavs Praudins was born on 30 January 1899 and became an officer in the Latvian Army. In 1941 he volunteered to serve under the Germans and from 13 January 1941 led *Schutzmannschafts* Battalion 19 with the rank of *Hauptmann*. During an inspection of the front near Krasnoye Selo, Praudins became involved in a heated dispute with *SS-Obergruppenführer* Jeckeln, the Senior SS and Police Commander "Russia North and Ostland", as a result of which Praudins was relieved on 7 August 1942. Initially sentenced to death (sic!), after intervention by Latvian politicians his sentence was commuted to five years imprisonment on 11 February 1943. This was later suspended so that he could prove himself at the front. He rehabilitated himself while serving as a simple grenadier in SS Volunteer Grenadier Regiment 39 (Latvian No.1). During the reorganization of the Latvian SS Volunteer Brigade into the 19th Latvian Volunteer Division, in January 1944 Praudins was assigned to the newly-formed I Battalion, Volunteer Grenadier Regiment 44 (Latvian No.6). Restored to his previous rank, he then commanded the I Battalion. On 16 January 1945 he assumed command of the entire regiment and was promoted to *Waffen-Sturmbannführer*. That same day he was awarded the German Cross in Gold. Praudins was arrested by Soviet troops on 5 June 1945 and was held as a forced laborer until 1961. After returning to Riga, he worked as a technical draftsman until his death on 9 October 1965.

***Waffen-Sturmbannführer* Voldemars Reinholds, 28/11/1944**
Voldemar Reinholds was born in Latvia on 23 June 1903 and served in the Latvian Army as an officer. As a *Legions-Hauptsturmführer*, on 11 November 1943 he was placed in command of III Battalion, SS Volunteer Grenadier Regiment 42. In August he took over the I Battalion in the same regiment. Promoted to *Waffen-Sturmbannführer*, he was awarded the German Cross in Gold[52] on 28 November 1944. In March 1945 he took over SS Waffen Grenadier Regiment 43. After the war he hid out in Latvia, but on 21 August 1948 he was arrested and sentenced to 25 years in the Workuta labor camp for serving with the Germans. His sentence was commuted in 1958 and he returned to Riga, where he worked as an electrician until 1977. He died in Madliena on 4 July 1986.

***SS-Obersturmführer* Walter Scheithauer, 12/09/1944**
SS-Obersturmführer Walter Scheithauer was awarded the German Cross in Gold on 12 September 1944.

---

52 A supposed awarding of the Knight's Cross could not be verified.

Approximately 3,000 Latvian members of the Waffen-SS
were killed during the Second World War.

Waffen-Hauptsturmführer **Georgs Seibelis, 29/01/1945**
Georgs Seibelis was born in Riga on 13 February 1913 and studied engineering, specializing in building construction. In the Latvian Army he reached the rank of lieutenant and was an instructor of non-commissioned officers and officer candidates. After Latvia was occupied by the Soviets in June 1940, he was sentenced to death but later managed to escape during a German bombing raid and fled to the partisans. When recruiting began, he volunteered immediately and was sent to a *Schutzmannschafts* battalion and saw action at Leningrad. Taken into the Latvian SS Volunteer Legion, in July 1943 Seibelis was promoted to *Legions-Obersturmführer* and made a company commander. In April 1944 he was promoted to *Legions-Hauptsturmführer* and given command of II Battalion, SS Volunteer Grenadier Regiment 42. Awarded the German Cross in Gold on 29 January 1945, after the war Seibelis tried to hide out in the forest. He was apprehended by Soviet troops, however, and sentenced to twenty years in a labor camp in Siberia. After sixteen years he returned to Riga physically broken and died there in 1970.

Waffen-Obersturmführer **Paulis Sprincis, 28/02/1945**
Paulis Sprincis was born in Grasi (Modohn District) on 10 April 1912 and from 1930 to 1934 studied economics. After completing his military service he decided on a career as an officer, which ended when the Red Army marched into Latvia in 1940. At the beginning of 1943 he volunteered to serve in the Latvian SS Volunteer Legion and on 11 July 1943 was made a *Legions-Untersturmführer*. While serving in SS Fusilier Battalion 19, on 21 June 1944 Sprincis was promoted to *Waffen-Obersturmführer*. He was awarded the German Cross in Gold on 28 February 1945. After the war he emigrated to Australia and died in Brisbane on 1 October 2006.

Waffen-Sturmbannführer **Eduards Stipnieks, 12/09/1944**
Eduards Stipnieks was born in Lozberge (Walk District) on 23 February 1902. In 1923 he joined the military and became a career soldier. In 1928 he completed officer training and until 17 June 1940 served in the Latvian 2nd Infantry Regiment. He was a member of the Territorial Corps until 21 June 1941 and subsequently fought against the Red Army as a partisan. From 16 July 1941 to 28 February 1942 Stipnieks worked as an insurance salesman and then joined *Schutzmannschafts* Battalion 24 as a company commander. In May 1943 he was taken into the Latvian SS Volunteer Legion as a *Legions-Hauptsturmführer*. He was later promoted to *Waffen-Sturmbannführer* in SS Waffen Grenadier Regiment 43 with an effective date of 21 June 1944. On 12 September 1944 Stipnieks was awarded the German Cross in Gold. After the war, he emigrated to Australia and died in Adelaide on 9 November 1983.

Waffen-Obersturmführer **Peteris Ziedainis, 08/05/1945**
Peteris Ziedainis was born in Novosibirsk on 15 January 1915, the son of Latvian parents. He and his family moved back to Jaunjelgava in 1920. In 1933 he began studying natural science and four years later did his military service. In 1937 he began a career as an officer and in September 1939 served in the Latgalian Artillery Regiment. One year later he transferred from the army to the air force and took flight training in Riga. After the German occupation he volunteered for military service and joined *Schutzmannschafts* Battalion 16. Ziedainis subsequently moved to the Latvian SS Volunteer Legion with the rank of *Legions-Untersturmführer* and on 30 January 1944 was promoted to *Legions-Obersturmführer*. He went on to command the 13th Company of SS Waffen Grenadier Regiment 42 and was presumably awarded the German Cross in Gold on 8 May 1945. After the surrender he procured false papers under the name Augusts Petersons and for a brief period led a partisan unit against the Red Army. On 5 October 1945 he was arrested by the Soviet secret police and was shot on 13 July 1946.

German Cross in Silver

19th SS Waffen Grenadier Division (Latvian No.2)

SS-Sturmbannführer **Hermann Lüdke, 25/01/1945**
Hermann Lüdke was born on 19 February 1910 and served in SS Motorized Infantry Regiment 4 as an *SS-Untersturmführer*. He was promoted to *SS-Sturmbannführer* on 25 March 1944. In the 19th SS Waffen Grenadier Division (Latvian No.2) he served as 2nd General Staff Officer and quartermaster and was responsible for the division's supply. For his work (including evacuation of the wounded, prisoners, damaged equipment) he was awarded the German Cross in Silver on 25 January 1945.

Army Honor Roll Clasp

15th SS Waffen Grenadier Division (Latvian No.1)

Waffen-Sturmbannführer **Vilis Hazners, 15/08/1944**
Vilis Hazners was born in Vircava (German Würzau, approx. 12 km S of Jelgava) on 23 July 1905. On 28 May 1943 he joined the Latvian SS Volunteer Legion as a *Legions-Hauptsturmführer* and on 24 June 1944 was promoted to *Waffen-Sturmbannführer*. After commanding I Battalion, SS Volunteer Grenadier Regiment 32 (Latvian No.3), in January 1945 he took over SS Fusilier Battalion 19. Hazners was awarded the Army Honor Roll Clasp on 15 August 1944. He died on 12 May 1989.

19th SS Waffen Grenadier Division (Latvian No.2)

Waffen-Obersturmführer **Janis Berzins, 05/03/1945**
Janis Berzins was born in Latvia on 14 February 1920 and his military service included commanding the 2nd Company of SS Waffen Grenadier Regiment 42 "Voldemars Veiss" (Latvian No.5). On 5 March 1945 he was decorated with the Army Honor Roll Clasp. After the war he emigrated to Germany.

Waffen-Untersturmführer **Augusts Biters, 15/03/1945**
Augusts Biters was born in Latvia on 9 September 1916 and in 1943 he was drafted into SS Grenadier Training and Replacement Battalion 15. After completing the third course for Germanic officers at the Bad Tölz SS officer school on 12 March 1944, he was transferred to the 19th Latvian SS Volunteer Division as signals platoon leader with the rank of *SS-Standarten-Oberjunker der Reserve*. On 30 June 1944 Biters was appointed *Waffen-Untersturmführer* and given command of 4th Company, SS Waffen Grenadier Regiment 44 (Latvian No.6). He was decorated with the Army Honor Roll Clasp on 5 March 1945.

Waffen-Oberscharführer **Janis Dzenis, 05/02/1945**
Janis Dzenis was born in Latvia and served in the Latvian Army as a non-commissioned officer. In 1943 he joined the Latvian SS Volunteer Legion and later served in I Battalion, SS Waffen Grenadier Regiment 43 (Latvian No.2). Dzenis was decorated with the Army Honor Roll Clasp on 5 February 1945. It is believed that he emigrated to Australia (Melbourne) after the war.

Waffen-Obersturmführer **Teodors Kalnajs, 10/04/1945**
Teodors Kalnajs was born in Laidze (Talsi District) in 1915 and served in the Latvian Army's 1st Guard Regiment in Talsi. At the end of 1941 he volunteered and was made a platoon leader in *Schutzmannschafts* Battalion 24. Taken into the 2nd Latvian SS Volunteer Brigade, he was wounded in action. After recovering from his wounds

he was placed in charge of the 8th Company of SS Volunteer Grenadier Regiment 44 (Latvian No.6) with the rank of *Waffen-Untersturmführer*. Promoted to *Waffen-Obersturmführer*, he served as aide-de-camp in the headquarters staff of SS Waffen Grenadier Regiment 44. On 10 April 1945 he was decorated with the Army Honor Roll Clasp. Kalnajs died in Laidze in 2007.

Waffen-Hauptsturmführer Ernests Laumanis, 05/03/1945
Ernests Laumanis was born in Libau on 18 May 1908 and attended the Latvian Military Academy. He joined *Schutzmannschafts* Battalion 21, later taking over its 1st Company. In October 1943 he commanded 1st Company, SS Volunteer Grenadier Regiment 42 as a *Legions-Untersturmführer*. Promoted to *Waffen-Hauptsturmführer*, he led SS Fusilier Battalion 19. On 5 March 1945 he was decorated with the Army Honor Roll Clasp. After the surrender Laumanis was sentenced to twenty years forced labor. Following his return to Latvia he worked in a sugar factory. Laumanis died in Mitau on 13 December 1968.

Waffen-Hauptsturmführer Janis Ozols, 25/02/1945
Janis Ozols was born on 28 April 1904 and served in the Latvian Army as an artilleryman. He volunteered in 1941 and joined the 1st Latvian Security Battalion "Riga", which on 5 February 1942 was renamed *Schutzmannschafts* Battalion 16. He initially led the battalion's 4th Company, from September 1942 the 1st Company, and finally in February 1943 the entire battalion for a short time. When the Latvian SS Volunteer Legion was formed, he took command of the 15th (Infantry Gun) Company of SS Volunteer Regiment 1. In 1944, with the rank of *Legions-Obersturmführer*, he was placed in command of 2nd Battery, SS Volunteer Artillery Regiment 19. After promotion to *Waffen-Hauptsturmführer*, Ozols led the III Battalion of SS Waffen Artillery Regiment 19 (Latvian No.2). On 25 February 1945 he was awarded the Army Honor Roll Clasp. Ozols died on 13 October 1947.

Waffen-Untersturmführer Vilhelm Piterans, 15/02/1945
Vilhelm Piterans was born in Latvia in 1916 and served in the Latvian Army as a non-commissioned officer. He came to the Latvian SS Volunteer Legion by way of the *Schutzmannschaften*, serving in SS Volunteer Regiment 2 (Latvian SS Volunteer Brigade). Promoted to *Waffen-Untersturmführer*, he ultimately commanded the 2nd Company of SS Waffen Grenadier Regiment 43 *"Hinrich Schuldt"*. On 15 February 1945 Piterans was awarded the Army Honor Roll Clasp for his service. He is believed to have been executed by the Red Army at the end of the war.

Waffen-Obersturmführer Gustavs Praudins, 07/01/1945
See biography under winners of the German Cross in Gold.

Knight's Cross of the Iron Cross[53]

15th SS Waffen Grenadier Division (Latvian No.1)

Waffen-Obersturmbannführer **Karlis Aperats, 21/09/1944**
Karlis Aperats was born in Riga (Latvia) on 4 March 1892 and in 1915 was drafted into the Russian Army. Transferred to the Latvian Rifle Regiment 1 in Daugavgrīva, he fought against German forces in the Riga area from 23 December 1916 until the end of August 1917 and on 26 January 1917 was made an NCO for bravery in the face of the enemy. After falling seriously ill, Aperats was discharged from the army on 19 December 1917. On 24 January 1919, however, he joined Latvian-German units which drove the Red Army from the country. He remained in military service and on 29 August 1919 was promoted to second lieutenant, on 10 January 1920 to first lieutenant and on 10 January 1924 to captain. When the Red Army again occupied the country in 1940, Aperats, by then a lieutenant colonel, joined the resistance. After the start of "Operation Barbarossa", on 3 August 1941 he was placed in charge of the Latvian Home Defense and on 30 August 1942 moved over to active service. He initially commanded *Schutzmannschafts* Battalion 26 and from March 1943 *Schutzmannschafts* Battalion 19. With that battalion Aperats moved to the Latvian SS Volunteer Legion and later commanded SS Waffen Grenadier Regiment 32 (Latvian No.1) with the rank of *Waffen-Obersturmbannführer*. Severely wounded on 16 July 1944, he committed suicide near Mosuli (Opochka area). Hitler awarded him the Knight's Cross posthumously on 21 September 1944.

SS-Oberführer **Nikolaus Heilmann, 23/08/1944**
See biography under division commanders.

19th SS Waffen Grenadier Division (Latvian No.2)

Waffen-Hauptsturmführer **Miervaldis Adamsons, 25/01/1945**
Miervaldis Adamsons was born in Poltava (Russia) on 29 June 1910 and after resettling in Latvia he briefly studied theology at the university in Riga (1928-29). He joined the merchant marine and later the French Foreign Legion. There he was promoted to sergeant and was twice decorated for bravery. After returning from Morocco, Adamsons joined the Latvian Army and served in the 8th Dvinsk Infantry Regiment. In June 1941 he volunteered to serve under the Germans and in June 1942 arrived in the Minsk area with *Schutzmannschafts* Battalion 26. In April 1943 he was taken into the 2nd Latvian SS Volunteer Brigade with the rank of *Legions-Untersturmführer*. He later commanded the 6th Company of SS Waffen Grenadier Regiment 44 (Latvian No.6) and was promoted to *Waffen-Obersturmführer*. On 1 September 1944 Adamsons was promoted to *Waffen-Hauptsturmführer*. He was severely wounded on 25 January 1945 and spent the rest of the war in a hospital in Libau. Adamsons was awarded the Knight's Cross on 25 January 1945. He was captured by the Soviets in Libau and was forced to work in nickel mines near Murmansk. He twice attempted to escape and was subsequently executed on 23 August 1948.

---

53 Several more Knight's Cross award recommendations were submitted and processed by the Army Personnel Office without the decoration being awarded. In the literature these award recommendations are considered proof that a decoration was in fact awarded. As a result, a number of persons have been identified as winners of the Knight's Cross even though they were not in fact decorated with this high-ranking medal.

Waffen-Obersturmführer Roberts Ancans, 25/01/1945
Roberts Ancans was born in Talsi on 11 November 1919 and in 1939-40 did his military service in the Latvian Army. He volunteered to serve in the *Schutzmannschaften* in the summer of 1942 and in February 1943 moved to the Latvian Legion. Ancans became leader of SS Field Replacement Battalion 19's division combat school, and on 25 January 1945 he was awarded the Knight's Cross and promoted to the rank of *Waffen-Obersturmführer*. After the war he resettled in the USA and died in New York on 1 January 1982.

Waffen-Hauptscharführer Zanis Ansons, 16/01/1945
Zanis Ansons was born in Kandava on 4 December 1912 and in 1942 volunteered to serve with the Germans. He was inducted into *Schutzmannschafts* Battalion 24 and in March 1943 was taken into the Latvian SS Volunteer Legion. On 1 October 1943 he was promoted to *Legions-Oberscharführer* and on 20 April 1944 to the rank of *Legions-Hauptscharführer*. At the same time he took over a platoon in 3rd Company, SS Volunteer Grenadier Regiment 44 (Latvian No.6). Ansons was awarded the Knight's Cross on 16 January 1945. After the surrender he was captured by the Soviets. He died in Kandava on 24 November 1968.

Waffen-Hauptsturmführer Zanis Butkus, 21/09/1944
Zanis Butkus was born in Augustkalne on 29 July 1906 and after completing school worked on his parent's farm. He served in the Latvian Army from 1927 to 1929 and as a particularly good rifle shot took part in many Latvian and Baltic competitions. During the Soviet occupation in 1940-41 his wife and daughter were sent to Siberia. Butkus himself joined the partisan movement and then entered German service. On 28 June 1944, while a *Waffen-Untersturmführer* in 10th Company, SS Waffen Grenadier Regiment 43, he was awarded the German Cross in Gold. Promoted to *Waffen-Hauptsturmführer*, on 25 January 1945 he was decorated with the Knight's Cross while commander of 10th Company, SS Field Replacement Battalion 19. Butkus emigrated to the USA and died in Palmer, Alaska on 15 May 1999.

Waffen-Obersturmführer Andrejs Freimanis, 05/05/1945
Andrejs Freimanis was born in Grobin (Libau District) on 21 December 1914. He joined the Latvian Army in 1934 and in 1938 achieved the rank of lieutenant. After entering German service, on 24 May 1943 he reached the rank of *Legions-Untersturmführer* and when the war ended commanded the 13th Company of SS Waffen Grenadier Regiment 44 with the rank of *Waffen-Obersturmführer*. On 5 May 1945 he was awarded the Knight's Cross. Butkus died in Frauenburg on 15 September 1994.

Waffen-Obersturmbannführer Nikolajs Galdins, 25/01/1945
See biography under winners of the German Cross in Gold.

Waffen-Unterschar*führer* Alfreds Riekstins, 05/04/1945
Alfreds Riekstins was born in Matkule on 30 January 1913 and in 1942 joined *Schutzmannschafts* Battalion 24. In May 1943 he moved to the Latvian SS Volunteer Brigade. Subsequently promoted to *Waffen-Unterscharführer* and assigned to 1st Company, SS Fusilier Battalion 19, he was awarded the Knight's Cross on 5 April 1945. When the war ended Riekstins fled to Sweden. There he was recruited by the British Secret Service and on 30 August 1952 was dropped into Latvia. Betrayed, on 11 September 1952 Riekstins committed suicide before he could be arrested by the NKVD.

SS-Gruppenführer and *Generalleutnant* der Waffen-SS Bruno Streckenbach, 27/08/1944(701st Oak Leaves), 16/01/1945
See biography under Division commanders.

Voldemars Veiss, the former head of security in the domestic administration of Latvia, was appointed *Legions-Standartenführer* on 1 August 1943. He was awarded the Knight's Cross on 9 February 1944,

As infantry commander of the 19th Latvian SS Volunteer Division, Veiss was badly wounded at the Velikaya River and died in hospital in Riga on 16 April 1944. His coffin, covered with the German military flag, was transported through Riga to the cemetery on a Sd.Kfz.124 Wespe.

Legions-Oberführer **Voldemars Veiss, 09/02/1944**
Voldemars Veiss was born in Riga on 7 November 1899 and became an officer in the Latvian Army. He achieved the rank of second lieutenant on 29 May 1919 and was promoted to first lieutenant in 1920. Veiss would have to wait fifteen years for promotion to captain, however! In April 1937 he became a lieutenant colonel in the general staff and in 1939 served as military attaché in Finland and Estonia. When Germany invaded the Soviet Union he set up an auxiliary police force under the German administration, from which the *Schutzmannschafts* battalions were formed soon afterwards. At the end of 1941 Veiss became Deputy Director-General of the Interior[54] and Director of Security in the domestic administration of Latvia. When the Latvian SS Volunteer Legion was formed, Veiss (a *Legions-Obersturmbannführer* since 1 April 1943) took command of SS Volunteer Regiment 1. On 1 August 1943 he was promoted to *Legions-Standartenführer* and named infantry commander of the Latvian SS volunteer Brigade. For his command of the Latvian grenadiers he was awarded the Knight's Cross on 9 February 1944. Severely wounded at the Velikaya River, Veiss died in hospital in Riga on 16 April 1944.

ORGANIZATION OF AN INFANTRY DIVISION 43

Planned Strength: 17,193 Men

Division Headquarters	173 men
3 grenadier regiments (3 battalions each)	9,179 men
Artillery Regiment	2,536 men

    I Battalion [1st – 3rd Batteries (105-mm light field howitzers)]
    II Battalion [4th – 6th Batteries (105-mm light field howitzers)]
    III Battalion [7th – 9th Batteries (105 mm light field howitzers)]
    IV Battalion [10th – 12th Batteries (150-mm heavy field howitzers)]

Fusilier Battalion/Reconnaissance Battalion	411 men
3 fusilier companies (1 on bicycles)	
1 heavy fusilier company	
Anti-Tank Battalion	555 men
Pioneer Battalion	642 men
4 companies (1 on bicycles)	
Signals Unit	440 men
1 company (telephone)	
1 company (radio)	
Supply Officer	2,443 men
3 workshop companies	
1 supply company	
9 small supply columns	
3 large supply columns	
Administration Services	212 men
1 bakery company	
1 butcher company	
1 rations office	
Medical Battalion	368 men
2 first-aid companies	
1 ambulance company	
Veterinary Company	234 men

---

54 He was hereby the deputy of Oskars Dankers, who had been appointed Director General of the Interior in the Latvian self-government in the General Commissariat *"Ostland"*.

Rank Comparisons

SS Rank	Foreign Rank	Army
SS-Grenadier	Waffen-Grenadier	Grenadier
SS-Sturmmann	Waffen-Sturmmann	Gefreiter
SS-Rottenführer	Waffen-Rottenführer	Obergefreiter
SS-Unterscharführer	Waffen-Unterscharführer	Unteroffizier
SS-Scharführer	Waffen-Scharführer	Unterfeldwebel
SS-Oberscharführer	Waffen-Oberscharführer	Feldwebel
SS-Hauptscharführer	Waffen-Hauptscharführer	Oberfeldwebel
SS-Untersturmführer	Waffen-Untersturmführer	Leutnant
SS-Obersturmführer	Waffen-Obersturmführer	Oberleutnant
SS-Hauptsturmführer	Waffen-Hauptsturmführer	Hauptmann
SS-Sturmbannführer	Waffen-Sturmbannführer	Major
SS-Obersturmbannführer	Waffen-Obersturmbannführer	Oberstleutnant
SS-Standartenführer	Waffen-Standartenführer	Oberst
SS-Oberführer	Waffen-Oberführer	no comparable rank
SS-Brigadeführer	Waffen-Brigadeführer	Generalmajor
SS-Gruppenführer	Waffen-Gruppenführer	Generalleutnant
SS-Obergruppenführer	Waffen-Obergruppenführer	General
SS-Oberstgruppenführer	—	Generaloberst

Suggested Reading

Dellin, Alexander, *Deutsche Herrschaft in Russland*, Düsseldorf, 1958
Haupt, Werner, *Heeresgruppe Nord*, Bad Nauheim, 1966
Haupt, Werner, *Kurland*, Dorheim, 1984
Kurowski, Franz, *Endkampf um das Reich*, Friedberg, 1987
Müller, G., *Die Geschichte der 207. und 281. Infanterie-Division*, Dortmund, 1958
Michaelis, Rolf, *Die Waffen-SS: Mythos und Wirklichkeit*, Berlin, 2006
Neulen, Werner, *An deutscher Seite*, München, 1985
Rürup, Reinhard, *Der Krieg gegen die Sowjetunion 1941-1945*, Berlin, 1991
Scheibert, Horst, *Die Träger des Deutschen Kreuzes in Gold*, Friedberg
Scherzer, Veit, *Ritterkreuzträger 1939-1945*, Jena, 2007
Schramm, Percy, *Kriegstagebuch des OKW 1940-1945*, München, 1982
Stöber, Hans, *Die lettischen Divisionen*, Osnabrück, 1981
Thorwald, Jürger, *Die Illusion*, Zürich, 1974
Die Wehrmachtberichte, Muunchen, 1985

Other Books by Rolf Michaelis

SS-Heimwehr Danzig in Poland 1939

SS-Fallschirmjäger-Bataillon 500/600

The 10th SS-Panzer-Division "Frundsberg"

The 11th SS-Freiwilligen-Panzer-Grenadier-Division "Nordland"

The 32nd SS-Freiwilligen-Grenadier-Division: "30.Januar"

Combat Operations of the German Ordnungspolizei, 1939-1945: Polizei-Bataillone • SS-Polizei-Regimenter

Cavalry Divisions of the Waffen-SS

Panzergrenadier Divisions of the Waffen-SS

The Kaminski Brigade

Belgians in the Waffen-SS

The German Sniper Badge 1944-1945

The German Tank Destruction Badge in World War II